God's Divine Plan

For His

Glorious Church

A Brief Insight

I0164742

Lonnie Brown

COPYRIGHT

ISBN: 978-0-615-85776-3

This Book is also available on AMAZON KINDLE – via AMAZON.COM

DEDICATION

This book is dedicated to all those who stood by me over the year and encouraged me in the Lord

CONTENTS

ACKNOWLEDGEMENTS

I wish to acknowledge the inspiration and insight I received from the Holy Spirit while studying the writings from Andrew Murray, William Law, R.A, Torrey, T.L. Osborn and Saint Ambrose. These writings were catalysts in which, through the Holy Spirit, made scriptural Truths come more alive to me. I am still studying and learning. There is so much wonderful Spiritual Truth to be had, that I believe it takes a lifetime just to come to the Spiritual understanding that God has for us here on Earth. The rest we will learn when we are finally home in heaven.

INTRODUCTION

My Search for the Truth

For many years I have been researching Church history, including the "why" things are the way they are and how the Early Church and Christians lived. Also I deeply searched for God's Divine Plan for His Church. R.A. Torrey says that no one can teach us the Truth like the Holy Spirit can. He also emphasized that we should learn from those who have been taught by God and His Holy Spirit. I now know this to be true.

Torrey, Andrew Murray, Saint Ambrose, William Law, T.L. Osborn and many others repeat the Truth, which the Holy Spirit revealed to them, over and over again in their writings. I have found this to be a good thing and do the same in this book. There is a Russian idiom which translates "Repetition is the mother of all learning." This too I know to be true, because when I was in sales, the more I repeated the sales pitch, the easier it became to remember and to this day, I can remember nearly all of it. Therefore, the Truth is repeated herein to help you remember it.

It would be easy for me to give just a synopsis of what I had learned, but that would be unfair to those of you who are seeking the same answers as I have been doing. Thus I have chosen to make this book a brief insight into God's Divine Plan for His Glorious Church. Each factual statement is supported by either scripture or by writings from Godly men, who all have experienced what I am sharing herein. Again this book is primarily written for seekers and those who desire more of God and the Holy Spirit in their life and in their church. I pray that those who read this book will not only research the information provided, but will also ask the Holy Spirit to teach them and reveal to them the Divine Truth. It is with the Holy Spirit's leading that I humbly write this.

Lonnie Brown
Author

CHAPTER 1: THE CHURCH – THE GLORIOUS BRIDE OF CHRIST

"even as Christ also loved the church, and gave himself for it;

26 That he might sanctify and cleanse it with the washing of water by the word,

27 That he might present it to himself a glorious church, not having spot, or wrinkle, or any such thing; but that it should be holy and without blemish." Ephesians 5:25-27

God, Jesus and the Holy Spirit Share the Same Divine Plan for the Church

God's plan for the Church (the Body of Christ) has always been a Glorious and Holy Church, without spot or wrinkle or anything that would make it unholy. However, throughout the centuries, self- righteous, pious and so called religious men and whose hearts have been hardened against the Truth, created their own non-scriptural religious beliefs. Their heretical beliefs are based on human reason, intellectual knowledge, pride and arrogance. Further they have made every attempt to replace **TRUE CHRISTIANITY** with their various worldly and devil inspired polluted doctrines. Over the centuries, their personal unscriptural opinions, false teachings and self-seeking desires, have caused the Church to end up splintering into many factions and denominations. Even though the Church appears to be divided more than ever today, it does not change the fact that God has always had a people, a remnant, which has stayed true to Him and His Word. Personally I have discovered this to be true in nearly every church that I have attended. Without a doubt, there remains a visible and invisible True Church (i.e., Body of Christ). This True Church is filled with God's love and the Holy Spirit's power. It is called the Church Triumphant.

Religion vs. Reality

Religion is "man seeking God or the Truth" and True Christianity is "God, Who is the Truth, seeking man." Brother Andrew Murray points out that in the Garden of Eden, Adam and Eve were given the opportunity to obey and trust God for everything. They were never told not to eat from "the Tree of Life", but were clearly warned not to eat from "the Tree of Knowledge."[1] God warned them that on the day that they did eat from it, they would surely die. The tree of "Life", on the other hand, offered them eternal life with God through trust and obedience. If they had not disobeyed and had chosen this

---

[1] Spirit of Christ, Andrew Murray, Kindle E-book

tree instead, God, in return would have continued to take care of them and would have supplied their every need. Sin, sickness and death would have not entered in the world. Yet, as we know they chose "the tree of Knowledge" due to the devil's (i.e. serpent's) enticement and lie that "God didn't mean what He said." As a result, their choice meant turning their world over to Satan and his deceptive and destructive lies. It was their decision not to trust and obey God that brought sin and suffering into the world. The world today, still seeks its own way.

Religion today makes that same enticing offer that "knowledge" is the pathway to God. Further, Religion binds its followers and teaches that they must strive and struggle to please God in order to win His love and receive eternal life. Religion also teaches that, pain, suffering, sickness and disease are all blessings that draw us closer to God. Through these lies the world and the devil have struck a great blow against the Church and the Gospel message. However, they have failed to wipe out True Christianity and the True Body of Christ. The Church Triumphant is still growing and going.

The Beginning of the Church

Nearly all Christian faiths agree that the Church began on the Day of Pentecost, when God sent His Holy Spirit to Earth in such a mighty way and that the Holy Spirit was outpoured in power, upon those prayerfully seeking God in the Upper Room in Jerusalem We read in the Book of Acts on how the disciples were filled with Divine love, Divine power and a new boldness. From that point on they were no longer the timid, arguing or doubting men that we read about in the preceding Gospels. In the first day alone, the Church grew by 3,000 and then later by 5,000 people, due to the Holy Spirit's outpouring of power.[2] Also in Acts we read about the Church's continuing growth under the Holy Spirit's power, with signs, wonders and miracles following. Plus we see that soon thereafter persecution, by both the religious leaders and the world rose rapidly against the Church. Self-righteous religious men elevated themselves and began teaching heresies and false doctrines. Such persecution only caused the Church to increase that much more. Persecution could not and cannot stop the Church or the Holy Spirit's power.

The Church today still needs the Holy Spirit's power. Without the Holy Spirit it is impossible to fulfill God's Divine Plan for His Church. Without the Holy Spirit there is no Church! Without the Holy Spirit there is no Christian life.

A Place of Healing and Restoration

We never know when someone will walk into our church that is on the verge of committing suicide or who is looking for a reason not to do it. We also seldom know the mental stress that someone is going through or who may be facing a divorce or who has just gone through a messy divorce and is looking for both answers and peace. We also need to

---

[2] Acts Chapter 2, 4, 5 and the entire Book of Acts

consider those, who enter our church, who are terribly gripped by sin and live in darkness and who are also seeking a way to be delivered from their darkness. There too are Christians who come to church, who are facing mental and spiritual battles and who may feel discouraged and defeated or have little hope left. Then there are also the sick and ailing, who not only need to hear that the Good News that God desires to heal them, but also need to have the Church Elders lay hands on them and pray for their healing. Only if more churches understood that God desires to heal people through them, more people would be healed. God's Divine Plan for His Church goes beyond our Sunday rituals and liturgies. The Church is to be a gathering place for God's children, where Agape love flows, healing and restoration take place, where the Holy Spirit is present and has freedom to move as He wills and where the Gospel is preached. God is still in the healing and saving business. The Church is to be in the same business.

When people walk into our church what will they actually see and hear? Will they hear the Good News that not only God loves them, but will they also hear that His Son Jesus Christ came to set them free from their sins and desires to heal them mentally, physically and spiritually? Will they find us filled and anointed with the Holy Spirit, His power, love and mercy? Or will they walk away in the same state as they came? The Church should and must be a place of healing, refuge and restoration. If it is not, then why do so many churches even exist?

The Gospel Message and Holy Spirit

It is through the Church (Body of Christ) that the message of salvation (i.e. the Gospel) is to be preached, taught and shared under the Holy Spirit's anointing. Such anointing will convict people of their sin and lead them to repentance and salvation. R.A. Torrey, in his book, "The Person and Work of the Holy Spirit" says that it is the work of the Holy Spirit is to convict the world of sin. He also says that the primary sin is the sin of unbelief that Jesus Christ is the Son of God. He gives examples of how it is impossible for us on our own, to convince someone of sin. No matter how hard we try, it is impossible. However, when we are filled with the Holy Spirit's power and are totally surrendered to Him, He then can minister and witness through us as well as give us the life giving words that someone needs to hear. We too, must know the reality of Jesus Christ through the Word of God. As we speak, the Holy Spirit will bring the right scriptures to our remembrance and make real the fact that Jesus lives in us. He will also convict that person of their need for Jesus and open their eyes to see that He is real. All the great men and women of God, which I have studied, down through the centuries, relied upon the Holy Spirit to minister through them. And when they did, thousands came to Christ, plus thousands were healed and delivered from the grip of the devil. Again, I must reiterate, without the Holy Spirit, we cannot be faithful and true witnesses for Christ. Without the Holy Spirit, one cannot be "Born Again." No one can be saved by "knowledge" alone.

God's Grace is revealed through the Holy Spirit

"Of how much sorer punishment, suppose ye, shall he be thought worthy, who hath trodden under foot the Son of God, and hath counted the blood of the covenant, wherewith he was sanctified, an unholy thing, and hath done despite unto the Spirit of grace?" Hebrews 10:29

"For through him we both have access by one Spirit unto the Father." Ephesians 2:18

"In whom ye also are builded together for an habitation of God through the Spirit." Ephesians 2:22

God does everything through Jesus and by the Holy Spirit. There are many books and scriptures on Grace. Yet, it is important to remember that when Grace is revealed to us, it is the Holy Spirit doing the revealing. The fact that He is called the Spirit of Grace proves that Grace comes through Him. As revealed in this book, the Holy Spirit convicts us of sin and leads us to Christ, plus the Holy Spirit is the One God uses to draw us to Himself. Saint Ambrose in his Books on the Holy Spirit proves by scripture that the Grace of the Father,

Son and Holy Spirit are the same Grace and that They work together in unison. None of them do anything secretly or contrary to each other. They are inseparable, even when it comes to Grace.

It also should be noted at this point that Grace is not cheap. Grace is costly because it cost Jesus Christ His life and shed blood. Grace doesn't give us license to keep on living sinful lives. Grace doesn't ignore our need for repentance, instead Grace is revealed by the Holy Spirit, which brings us to repentance. Even though God's Grace is available to all who will repent and surrender their life to Jesus, Grace does not pardon our sin until we repent of it and accept God's Grace. Grace cannot be earned or rewarded. The Spirit of Grace, which also is the Holy Spirit, can be rejected and sinned against by those who were once saved by Grace. Grace is Holy because God is Holy.

The Church is a Place where God's People Assemble

The Church is not a building or a cathedral. The word "Church" in the Greek means "assembly" or "called out." For nearly three centuries the Early Christians assembled together in homes, secret places, and perhaps in large rooms or wherever they could find a place. Church buildings and cathedrals didn't come into existence until the Fourth century. Even today, in persecuted countries, Christians often meet in secret in the same manner as the Early Christians met.

Gathering together for them is something they look forward to because they experience a great joy when they do. Although they know that they can be arrested, beaten, tortured, loose everything they own or even be killed for gathering together, they still choose to do it. The reason they risk everything is because Jesus means everything to them and He is in their midst when they do meet. Also they find gathering together equips them to be better living witnesses. On other hand, thousands in the free world shamefully consider Church as an option. Would you live for Jesus if it meant losing everything?

The Church is to be One Body

Prior to the cathedrals, the clergy (priests, bishops, elders and etc.) worshipped and ministered among the people. They were One Body and Community under the Holy Spirit's Supreme authority. The cathedrals originally were not designed to separate the people but to unify them. Unfortunately, church history has shown that many of these cathedrals became cold and spiritually dead places of worship. More than often, the Holy Spirit was replaced with knowledge, man-made traditions, liturgies and religious beliefs. There were clergy who elevated themselves above their brothers and sisters in the Lord. Sadly many still do today.

Nowhere in scripture does it allow a Spiritual leader to elevate himself or herself above the flock or take advantage of the flock.[3] The greater the leadership role, the greater the

---

[3] 1 Peter 5:1-4

servant one must be.[4] I met such a humble leader, who truly took on the role of a servant. This man was Metropolitan Jonah, who at that time was the head of the Orthodox Church of America. He had just conducted a liturgy and when church was over, I approached him and complimented him on his homily. He responded by simply bowing at his waist and saying, "Pray for me a sinner." His few words and actions astounded me. His humility and meekness proved that he had the heart of a servant. Oh if only every pastor would be this humble..

Paul and Peter wrote that we are to submit ourselves to our Spiritual leaders and to honor them with our gifts and offerings, as well as, that all of us, including the Spiritual leaders are to clothe ourselves with humility and to be subject to each other.[5] The Church is to be one body under Christ. It is only through the Holy Spirit that the Church can be one Body.

Reasons Why Churches Grow

A. Door-to-door evangelism;

B. Popularity of the Pastor or Church Programs;

C. A compromised or no Gospel message;

D. Traditional Doctrine and most of the Gospel Preached;

---

[4] Mark 10:42-44
[5] 1Timothy 5:17; 1 Peter 5:5; 1 Thessalonians 5:11-13

E. The Gospel message preached, plus the Holy Spirit's moving, as to where lives are being changed, people healed and delivered.

This is God's Divine Plan for His Glorious Church: that the Gospel Message be preached under the Holy Spirit's anointing, as to where lives are being transformed, people healed and delivered

Lest We Forget

We have a future, a "Blessed Hope", that someday we will be free from all the pain, sorrow, heartaches, trials and troubles we face in this life today. We have a future in which we will become immortal and deified, living in joy and peace, with all the other saints, Jesus, and the angels, plus we will eternally be in God's presence. The world around us distracts us and we get our eyes and our hope off of our future. Or we get so caught up in our religion, our beliefs or doing things for God, that we often forget our future. When things in life suddenly go wrong, our vision of heaven and eternity usually grows dim. There are days when we get discouraged and have trouble remembering that we will be included our Lord's heavenly glorious church. Yet my friends, allow me to encourage you not to give up hope. Our assurance lies in Jesus Christ. The Holy Spirit is the One who will instill in us that peace, joy and hope, which will encourage us to press on. Let us not forget that we are more than "conquerors" in Christ Jesus.

CHAPTER 2: BASIC FOUNDATIONAL BELIEFS

"¹⁵ He saith unto them, But whom say ye that I am?

¹⁶ And Simon Peter answered and said, Thou art the Christ, the Son of the living God.

¹⁷ And Jesus answered and said unto him, Blessed art thou, Simon Barjona: for flesh and blood hath not revealed it unto thee, but my Father which is in heaven.

¹⁸ And I say also unto thee, That thou art Peter, and upon this rock I will build my church; and the gates of hell shall not prevail against it." Matthew 16

The First Foundation: Jesus Christ is the Son of the Living God

The core of Christianity and the Gospel Message is the foundational Truth that Jesus Christ is the Son of the living God. Any other belief or teaching is an anti-Christ teaching and cannot be called either the Gospel or Christianity. This is what separates us from all other religions and beliefs in the World.

The Second Foundation: Jesus is the Only Way unto God

"Jesus saith unto him, I am the way, the truth, and the life: no man cometh unto the Father, but by me." John 14:6

"I am the door: by me if any man enter in, he shall be saved, and shall go in and out, and find pasture." John 10:9

"16 For God so loved the world, that he gave his only begotten Son, that whosoever believeth in him should not perish, but have everlasting life.

17 For God sent not his Son into the world to condemn the world; but that the world through him might be saved.

18 He that believeth on him is not condemned: but he that believeth not is condemned already, because he hath not believed in the name of the only begotten Son of God." John 3

Another anti-Christ doctrine, which is rapidly spreading around the world, is that "there are many paths to God." There is also the false teaching that if a person does nothing but good in his life he will make it to heaven. People generally believe that they are good, but they are deceived by their own heart:

> *"The heart is deceitful above all things, and desperately wicked: who can know it?" Jeremiah 17:9*

People want to believe that they can devise their own path and that as long as they are good and do right, or follow the rules of their religion, then that is all that is required of them in life. Yet, as we read in the preceding verses there is no other way unto God or salvation. And those who choose not to believe are condemned by God because of their unbelief. I have heard well-meaning Christians make excuses for those who are not Christian, that surely God would accept them for their goodness or for at least trying to do what is right. They simply don't know scripture.

> *"Neither is there salvation in any other: for there is none other name under heaven given among men, whereby we must be saved." Acts 4:12*

There is no other name under heaven, other than Jesus, by which men can be saved. Yet, people don't want to hear this. They want a god of comfort and convenience, someone who will not confront them about their sin, or make them feel guilty for the way they live their self-indulgent life. They say that God is love. What they mean is that God is love as long as He accepts their concept of Him. They simply don't want to be forced to serve God. "God compels no man to serve him."[6] Salvation is offered as a "free gift." Unlike some so called religions, no one is forced to believe in or serve God. People earn eternal death.[7]

The Third Foundation: The Church and Christianity are Built upon the Apostles, Prophets and Jesus

"For other foundation can no man lay than that is laid, which is Jesus Christ." I Cointhians. 3:11

"[18] For through him we both have access by one Spirit unto the Father.

[19] Now therefore ye are no more strangers and foreigners, but fellow citizens with the saints, and of the household of God;

[20] And are built upon the foundation of the apostles and prophets, Jesus Christ himself being the chief corner stone;

---

[6] Saint Innocent of Alaska
[7] Romans 3:23

²¹ In whom all the building fitly framed together groweth unto an holy temple in the Lord:

²² In whom ye also are builded together for an habitation of God through the Spirit." Ephesians. 2

Jesus is the corner stone of the Church's foundation, which is also built upon the Apostles and the Prophets. We are built together, and grow together upon this foundation, so that God can dwell in us through the Holy Spirit. A social or compromising gospel is not a true Christian foundation. A foundation built upon knowledge and philosophy is not a true Christian foundation. Just because some religions have the word "Christian" in them, doesn't make them Christian, especially if their foundation is built on anything else. False foundations are based on false premises, which usually come from twisted scriptural interpretations and people's illogical reasoning   . Jesus equates building such a foundation to that of: *"a foolish man, which built his house upon the sand:' Matt. 7:6*   Without Jesus Christ as the corner stone, there is no Church and no Christianity.

Our Basic Foundational Beliefs are found in "The Nicene Creed"

I believe in one God,
the Father Almighty,
maker of heaven and earth,
and of all things visible and invisible;

And in one Lord Jesus Christ,

the only begotten Son of God,

begotten of his Father before all worlds,

God of God, Light of Light,

very God of very God,

begotten, not made,

being of one substance with the Father;

by whom all things were made;

who for us men and for our salvation

came down from heaven,

and was incarnate by the Holy Ghost

of the Virgin Mary,

and was made man;

and was crucified also for us under Pontius Pilate;

he suffered and was buried;

and the third day he rose again

according to the Scriptures,

and ascended into heaven,

and sitteth on the right hand of the Father;

and he shall come again, with glory,

to judge both the quick and the dead;

whose kingdom shall have no end.

And I believe in the Holy Ghost the Lord, and Giver of Life,

who proceedeth from the Father [and the Son];

who with the Father and the Son together

is worshipped and glorified;

who spake by the Prophets.

And I believe one holy Catholic[8] and Apostolic Church;

I acknowledge one baptism for the remission of sins;
and I look for the resurrection of the dead,
and the life of the world to come. AMEN.[9]

What and In Whom We Believe Matters

Those who change or alter the foundational Truths given to us by the Holy Spirit and from the Word of God are presenting a different gospel. Even though heresy, as well as deceitful and prideful men have entered into the Church over the centuries, there remain the basic foundational truths. Men may have altered these truths, yet God's Spiritual Truths can never be changed. Those who seek God with their whole heart will find Him and via His Holy Spirit, He will teach them and reveal to them His Truth. God does not alter His Word. He does not bow down or succumb to man's interpretations or to human wisdom. If we do not know the Word of God and have not the Holy Spirit leading us every day, then we too can be deceived by "good sounding" and "logical" human reasoning. We must hold fast to the True foundational Beliefs. Only the Holy Spirit will teach us and confirms these truths to us. May we be willing to set aside our human wisdom and knowledge and allow the Holy Spirit to reveal God's Word and Truth to us. The Church and Christianity are built upon Jesus Christ, the Solid Rock.

---

[8] Universal Church, i.e. Body of Christ
[9] The Orthodox Christian version since 1549, used in various forms by Catholic and Protestant churches.

CHAPTER 3: THE CHURCH'S STRUCTURE AND OPERATION

Jesus is Head of the Church – His Body

"...*Christ is the head of the church: and he is the saviour of the body." Ephesians. 5:23 (in part)*

"...*the church is subject unto Christ..." Ephesians, 5:24 (in part)*

"...*Christ also loved the church, and gave himself for it;*

[26] *That he might sanctify and cleanse it with the washing of water by the word,*

[27] *That he might present it to himself a glorious church, not having spot, or wrinkle, or any such thing; but that it should be holy and without blemish." Eph. 5:25-27*

Paul, in his letter to the Ephesians, compares the holiness and sanctity of marriage with that of Jesus' role in being the Head (i.e. Bridegroom) of His Body - the Church. Take notice here, if you will, that Jesus also is the redeeming savior of His Body (we who are saved and Born Again.) In return, the Church (we) are to be fully submitted and subject unto Jesus, (Who does the Father's Will) and unto the Holy Spirit. In other words, we are to give our all unto Him and trust Him, through the Holy Spirit to take care of us. Through this submission, we are choosing to be His faithful Bride and to be obedient unto Him in all things and in doing so, we are showing forth our true love and devotion unto Him. Paul goes on to show that Jesus loved us so much that He willingly laid down His life for us, so that we may become His Holy Bride. By giving Himself freely, He is now able to sanctify and cleanse His Church so that it will be "glorious, without spot or wrinkle", as well as "Holy" and "without blemish." Stop, if you will for a moment and let this truth sink into your heart.

God is the Head of Jesus

"...the head of Christ is God." 1 Corinthians, 11:3 (in part).

Just as Jesus is Head of the Church, so is God Our Father is Head of Jesus. Jesus is eternally submitted unto the Father.

The Holy Spirit is the Supreme Authority in the Church

"... [T]he Holy Spirit is represented as the One who is the supreme authority in the church, who calls men to work and appoints them to office." [10]

[10] Torrey, R. A. (Reuben Archer) (2011-03-24). The Person and Work of The Holy Spirit (p. 10). . Kindle Edition.

"Now there were in the church that was at Antioch certain prophets and teachers; as Barnabas, and Simeon that was called Niger, and Lucius of Cyrene, and Manaen, which had been brought up with Herod the tetrarch, and Saul.

[2] As they ministered to the Lord, and fasted, the Holy Ghost said, Separate me Barnabas and Saul for the work whereunto I have called them.

[3] And when they had fasted and prayed, and laid their hands on them, they sent them away." Acts 13:1-3

Many a church has failed to pray and seek the Holy Spirit's direction, before they elected or appointed people to certain positions in the church and as a result, they often have ended up having some form of conflict. Only the Holy Spirit can give discernment and direction when it comes to confirming whom God has "Called" and Chosen for certain positions in the Church. This includes not only the leadership roles, but it also applies to appointing elders, deacons, teachers, laity positions and administrative duties. Each position should be carefully prayed over, by the Church and the leadership, before any appointment or election. This is how the Early Church operated.

God's Order of Hierarchy in the Church

"²⁷ Now you [collectively] are Christ's body and [individually] you are members of it, each part severally and distinct [each with his own place and function].

²⁸ So God has appointed some in the church [^[l]for His own use]: first apostles (special messengers); second prophets (inspired preachers and expounders); third teachers; then wonder-workers; then those with ability to heal the sick; helpers; administrators; [speakers in] different (unknown) tongues." 1 Corinthians 12:27-28 (Amplified Bible)

"¹¹ And His gifts were [varied; He Himself appointed and gave men to us] some to be apostles (special messengers), some prophets (inspired preachers and expounders), some evangelists (preachers of the Gospel, traveling missionaries), some pastors (shepherds of His flock) and teachers.

¹² His intention was the perfecting and the full equipping of the saints (His consecrated people), [that they should do] the work of ministering toward building up Christ's body (the church),

[13] *[That it might develop] until we all attain oneness in the faith and in the comprehension of the [[b]full and accurate] knowledge of the Son of God, that [we might arrive] at really mature manhood (the completeness of personality which is nothing less than the standard height of Christ's own perfection), the measure of the stature of the fullness of the Christ and the completeness found in Him: "Ephesians, 4:11-13 (Amplified Bible)*

"[4] For as in one physical body we have many parts (organs, members) and all of these parts do not have the same function or use,

[5] So we, numerous as we are, are one body in Christ (the Messiah) and individually we are parts one of another [mutually dependent on one another].

[6] Having gifts (faculties, talents, qualities) that differ according to the grace given us, let us use them: [He whose gift is] prophecy, [let him prophesy] according to the proportion of his faith;

[7] [He whose gift is] practical service, let him give himself to serving; he who teaches, to his teaching;

[8] He who exhorts (encourages), to his exhortation; he who contributes, let him do it in simplicity and

liberality; he who gives aid and superintends, with zeal and singleness of mind; he who does acts of mercy, with genuine cheerfulness and joyful eagerness." Romans 12 (Amplified Bible)

Paul makes it clear that we, in Christ, are all members of Christ's Body and that we are to be mutually dependent upon each other. Keeping this in mind, God's Plan for the Church begins with the Apostles, then prophets (Holy Spirit inspired preachers and expounders of the Word), evangelists (preachers and traveling missionaries), pastors (shepherds of His flock), teachers, miracles (wonder workers), gifts of healing those with ability to heal the sick), helpers (laity), governments (those with administrative capabilities) and diversity of tongues. This is the Spiritual Order that God Himself established. Everyone in the Body of Christ is to work together for the perfecting of one another (i.e. the Saints), for the work of ministry and for the edifying of the body of Christ and they are to do so under the anointing of the Holy Spirit. No matter what one's calling is or position in the Church, they need Jesus living in them and through them by the power and presence of the Holy Spirit. This is the only way that we may truly fulfill our part as the member of the Jesus' Body. Without the Holy Spirit we cannot do this.

Every Member of Christ's Body is to Be Filled with the Holy Spirit

Both Torrey and Andrew Murray, in their writings, reveal that God's Divine Plan for every member of the Body of Christ is to be filled with the Holy Spirit and surrendered to the moving and leading of the Holy Spirit. This is how the Body of Christ is able to have the "unity of faith." The Early Christians were submitted to the Holy Spirit which resulted in thousands continually being added to the Church. It was under the Holy Spirit's anointing that they had "Love" feasts and broke bread together. This Love was a Divine love that will be explained further in another chapter. However, imagine for a moment, if you will, everyone in the local church community being filled with the Holy Spirit and the Love of God. Would not the power and presence of the Lord be real? As we will see herein, this has always been God's Divine Plan for His Glorious Church. And that Plan is for us to be filled with all of Him.

CHAPTER 4: THE HOLY SPIRIT'S WORK IN THE LOCAL CHURCH COMMUNITY

Who Is the Holy Spirit?

Among Christians and Christian faiths there are controversies concerning the Holy Spirit, who He is and what He does. R.A. Torrey gives a true Biblical insight into who the Holy Spirit really is. He says that, "the Holy Spirit is a Divine Person, worthy to receive our adoration, our faith, our love, and our entire surrender to Himself,"[11] Torrey goes on to say, "if we once grasp the thought that the Holy Spirit is a Divine Person of infinite majesty, glory and holiness and power, who in marvellous condescension has come into our hearts to make His abode there and take possession of our lives and make use of them, it will put us in the dust and keep us in the dust."[12]

Sadly, not all churches teach this. For many, He is simply a Spirit or source of power. The belief that the Holy Spirit is a mere force, denies His Deity and Oneness with the Father and Son.[13] It is highly important to know Him as a Divine Person, who comes to dwell in our hearts. We know

---

[11] Torrey, R. A. (Reuben Archer) (2011-03-24). The Person and Work of The Holy Spirit (p. 4). . Kindle Edition.
[12] Ibid.
[13] Saint Ambrose, Book 1, On The Holy Spirit,

and believe that Jesus comes to dwell in our hearts. He does this by and through the Holy Spirit. Romans 8:11; Ephesians 3:17; and John 14:18. God is the one who sends Holy Spirit to dwell in us. The Holy Spirit, Father and Son are inseparable; therefore He too is a Divine person.[14]

The Holy Spirit Doesn't Do Our Bidding

"[T]he Holy Spirit is not a power that we get hold of and use according to our will but a Person of sovereign majesty, who uses us according to His will."[15]

"The Spirit like the wind is sovereign."

"He is sovereign—we cannot dictate to Him. He "divides to each man" severally even "as He will "

"[W]hile we cannot dictate to the Holy Spirit we can learn the laws of His operations and by bringing ourselves into harmony with those laws, above all by submitting our wills absolutely to His sovereign will, the sovereign Spirit of God will work through us and accomplish His own glorious work by our instrumentality."[16]

The Holy Spirit doesn't do our bidding or bend to our will and wishes. It is we, who must continually submit to His

---

[14] Ibid.

[15] Torrey, R. A. (Reuben Archer) (2011-03-24). The Person and Work of The Holy Spirit (p. 5). . Kindle Edition.

[16] Torrey, R. A. (Reuben Archer) (2011-03-24). The Person and Work of The Holy Spirit (p. 24). . Kindle Edition.

will so that He can freely move, live, minister and love through us. This is one of the reasons why many a church and Christians have failed; they want the Holy Spirit to be at their disposal when they need Him, or they try to limit Him and control Him. It will never happen. Jesus can only be our Master, when we have surrendered to the Mastership of the Holy Spirit. Without Him, it is impossible to please God.

Some believe that they can drum Him up and cause Him to move in their midst through their much emotional singing, praising, shouting and commanding. What usually happens is a lot of testosterone, hype and emotionalism is built up, which they claim is the Holy Spirit's moving. Dietrich Bonheoffer says that when people try to move ahead of God they are actually "dethroning the Holy Spirit." Those who are impatient with the way God and the Holy Spirit moves or think that they can force Him to perform signs, wonders and miracles, don't know Him. These individuals refuse to yield and repent of their spiritual pride and they also refuse to see or hear the Truth, which comes from the Holy Spirit and God's Word. The Holy Spirit moves mightily only through those who are fully yielded to Him. Sin, pride, self-righteousness, unforgiveness and the Holy Spirit don't mix. HE IS HOLY, AND MAKES HOLY, THOSE WHO REPENT AND YIELD UNTO HIM AND THE LORD. GOD NEVER COMPROMISES WHEN IT COMES TO HOLINESS.

The Secret behind Success in the Church and in Our Christian's Life

"Herein lies the whole secret of a real Christian life, a life of liberty and joy and power and fullness. To have as one's ever-present Friend, and to be conscious that one has as his ever-present Friend, the Holy Spirit and to surrender one's life in all its departments entirely to His control, this is true Christian living."[17]

We are taught that God wants all of us and that Jesus wants all of us. What we are not often taught is that the Holy Spirit wants all of us too. You see my friends; God and Jesus do nothing without the Holy Spirit. The Father, Son and Holy Spirit are inseparable; they work together.[18] Although the Holy Spirit has a Divine Purpose, He fulfills the Father's Will, the same as Jesus does. (There is much more to this, which is not the purpose of this book to go into full detail, but you may read about this in Torrey's book, and Andrew Murray's books listed in the Biography and Recommended Reading section in the back of this book.) I will say this again; without the Holy Spirit there is no Church and there is no Christian life. Do you know Him as your ever-present Friend?

---

[17] Ibid. (p. 13). . Kindle Edition.

[18] *Saint Ambrose, His Three Books on the Holy Spirit.*

We Can Only Come Before God through Jesus and By the Holy Spirit

"For through him we both have access by one Spirit unto the Father." Eph. 2:18

"Jesus saith unto him, I am the way, the truth, and the life: no man cometh unto the Father, but by me." John 14:6

"God is a Spirit: and they that worship him must worship him in spirit and in truth." John 4:24

Both Torrey and Murray point out in their books that God can only be approached in the Spirit and by the Holy Spirit, through Jesus Christ. While deceived men, over the centuries, have tried to get around this and through their own efforts have tried to approach the Throne of God through their written prayers and liturgies; they have never been able to enter into His presence without the Holy Spirit. God, out of mercy and grace, may have responded to some of their prayers, yet, they never have been able to enter into His presence without the leading of the Holy Spirit. The Holy Spirit is the Spirit of Truth. Only He can effectively pray through us in Truth, in Jesus name and only He can bring us into God's presence. There is no other way.

"Oh the Joy that Floods My Soul..."

"Oh the joy that floods my soul when I'm with You, Lord

When I'm with You, Lord

Oh the joy that floods my soul when I'm with You, Lord

When I'm with You, Lord."

Clayton Brooks – "Take Me In"[19]

Pastor Clayton, under the Holy Spirit's anointing, composed this song and chorus about his wonderful experience in being in the Lord's presence when he prays. It is only through the Holy Spirit that he is able to experience this overwhelming joy that floods his soul. Personally, I have known Pastor Clayton for many years, and I know that he truly is an anointed man of God. And I also know personally about the joy that he has expressed here in his song. You too can experience that joy. Ask the Holy Spirit to take you in to God's presence. He will do it.

You see my friends; there are Christians who believe that seeking God and spending time with Him is boring and too hard to do. But it is not, especially when you come before the Father, in Jesus name, and ask the Holy Spirit to pray through you. He will teach you how to wait before the Lord as He brings you into the presence of the Throne; where you will experience great, overflowing joy and peace. When He does, there will be no doubt in your heart or mind that you are in God's wonderful presence. Have you ever experienced God's presence when you pray?

---

[19] Brooks. Clayton, "Take Me In" 2013; from the Album "Lift Up the Light" http://www.theoaksonline.org/product/music-cd/oaks-worship-lift-up-the-light/

There is a presence and joy that we can experience every day by keeping our Lord's commandments:

> *"Jesus answered and said unto him, If a man love me, he will keep my words: and my Father will love him, and we will come unto him, and make our abode with him." John 14:23*

Do you not desire to have the joy that floods your soul?

We are to Encourage and Uplift One Another

> *"Let the word of Christ dwell in you richly in all wisdom; teaching and admonishing one another in psalms and hymns and spiritual songs, singing with grace in your hearts to the Lord." Colossians 3:16*

> *"Speaking to yourselves in psalms and hymns and spiritual songs, singing and making melody in your heart to the Lord;" Ephesians 5:19*

> *"Confess your faults one to another, and pray one for another, that ye may be healed. The effectual fervent prayer of a righteous man availeth much." James 5:16*

> *"And be ye kind one to another, tenderhearted, forgiving one another, even as God for Christ's sake hath forgiven you" Ephesians 4:32*

> *"Be kindly affectioned one to another with brotherly*

love; in honour preferring one another; Romans 12:10"

"A new commandment I give unto you, That ye love one another; as I have loved you, that ye also love one another." John 13:34

It is by the Holy Spirit that the Love of God is shed abroad in our hearts. The Word of Christ can only dwell in us richly in all wisdom by the Holy Spirit. Again it is through the Holy Spirit and in the name of Jesus that we are to teach and admonish one another. By the same Spirit we are to sing psalms, hymns, spiritual songs which the Holy Spirit gives us to sing, and we are to do it all with grace in our hearts to the Lord. It is through the Holy Spirit that we are able to be kind and have a tenderhearted Godly affection for one another and we are to do it tenderheartedly. Through the Holy Spirit and with the Love of God we are to forgive one another with brotherly love, honoring and preferring one another over ourselves. Praying for one another and confessing our faults to one another is to be done through the Holy Spirit's leading. Only He can lead us to the trusting brother or sister in Christ who will keep secret our confession and yet earnestly pray for us. We must rely upon the Holy Spirit when we gather together.

Music and Singing are Continuous in Heaven

Richard Sigmund in his book, "My Time In Heaven," tells about the glorious music he heard while he was in heaven. When people would sing the angels and saints would join in. Music in heaven is uplifting just as Holy Spirit inspired music and singing are uplifting here. That's why, by the Spirit, we are to sing psalms, hymns and spiritual songs when we gather together. Heavenly inspired music opens up our hearts and allows the joy of the Lord and the love of God to permeate our being. Unfortunately, there are songs and music that are not inspired by the Holy Spirit and are like dried bones in the dessert. There is a difference between singing what the Holy Spirit leads and inspires us to sing and what man thinks is best for us to sing. Even today, there are Christian musicians, who believe they can reach the world with compromising worldly music, which leaves out the mention of God or Jesus. I heard Vestal Goodman, (the queen of Southern Gospel) in an interview with Bill Gaither, say, "that if young people today don't write and play music inspired by the Holy Spirit, then they need to quit and get a job at a grocery store or something." We cannot win the world through compromise.

CHAPTER 5: SALVATION AND THE HOLY SPIRIT'S ANOINTING

Are There Many Paths to God?

The world around us seems to be moving at a faster pace in advocating tolerance towards all religions, as well as attempting to erase the lines of difference between them. Societies around the world have latched on to the theme that "there are many paths to God" and the idea that "since we all seek the same thing, we simply all need to get along." The shocking and sad part is that there are Christians and Christian faiths which have bought into these "heretical" deceptions. Logic, rationalization and good sounding reason have become the trump cards over foundational, sound Biblical doctrine and scriptures. Many don't realize that they are being duped into believing a satanic and antichrist doctrine designed to keep them from God and the Truth. Nor do they see that it is the same ploy used by the serpent in the Garden of Eden when he basically said, "God doesn't mean what He says." Therefore, this message is humbly written to expose the lie and reveal what God says. The Church must rise up and take a stand as it has since the beginning.

These False Doctrines Were Predicted

2 Timothy 4: 3 "*For the time is coming when [people] will not tolerate (endure) sound and wholesome instruction, but, having ears itching [for something pleasing and gratifying], they will gather to themselves one teacher after another to a considerable number, chosen to satisfy their own liking and to foster the errors they hold,*

4 And will turn aside from hearing the truth and wander off into myths and man-made fictions." (Amplified Bible).

When I was ten years old I heard John G. Hall, a Godly man who was well versed in scripture, tell about how in the Last Days false doctrines would arise denying that Jesus Christ was the only way unto God. Even though later on, I studied World religions when I was a student at ORU, I never imagined I would see and hear the bold satanic lies that are being propagated around the world today. Even more so, I find it very disturbing that churches and Christians have fallen for such deceptions. Especially since the scriptures make the Truth so plain and clear.

Saint John made it Perfectly Clear that there will be Those who Deny Jesus

"Boys (lads), it is the last time (hour, the end of this age). And as you have heard that the antichrist [he who will oppose Christ in the guise of Christ] is coming, even now many antichrists have arisen, which confirms our belief that it is the final (the end) time." 1 John 2:18;

"Who is [such a] liar as he who denies that Jesus is the Christ (the Messiah)? He is the antichrist (the antagonist of Christ), who [habitually] denies and refuses to acknowledge the Father and the Son." 1 John 2:22;

"And every spirit which does not acknowledge and confess that Jesus Christ has come in the flesh [but would annul, destroy, sever, disunite Him] is not of God [does not proceed from Him]. This [nonconfession] is the [spirit] of the antichrist, [of] which you heard that it was coming, and now it is already in the world. ⁴Little children, you are of God [you belong to Him] and have [already] defeated and overcome them [the agents of the antichrist], because He Who lives in you is greater (mightier) than he who is in the world." 1 John 4:3-4;

"For many imposters (seducers, deceivers, and false leaders) have gone out into the world, men who will not acknowledge (confess, admit) the coming of Jesus Christ (the Messiah) in bodily form. Such a one is the imposter (the seducer, the deceiver, the false leader, the antagonist of Christ) and the antichrist." 2 John 1:7. (Amplified Bible)

John made it perfectly clear that any doctrine that denies Jesus Christ (and that He is the only way to God) is the doctrine of the antichrist. Further he goes on to say that we are to separate ourselves and not associate with such people who proclaim this doctrine:

"9 Anyone who runs on ahead [of God] and does not abide in the doctrine of Christ [who is not content with what He taught] does not have God; but he who continues to live in the doctrine (teaching) of Christ [does have God], he has both the Father and the Son.

10 If anyone comes to you and does not bring this doctrine [is disloyal to what Jesus Christ taught], do not receive him [do not accept him, do not welcome or admit him] into [your] house or bid him Godspeed or give him any encouragement." 2 John 1"9-10. (Amplified Bible)

Even Saint Paul says that People will turn to Seducing Spirits

"But the [Holy] Spirit distinctly and expressly declares that in latter times some will turn away from the faith, giving attention to deluding and seducing spirits and doctrines that demons teach,

[2] Through the hypocrisy and pretensions of liars whose consciences are seared (cauterized)," 1 Timothy 4:1-2. (Amplified Bible).

The scriptures make it perfectly clear that doctrines and teachings of men that not only deny the Deity of Jesus Christ, why He came, or preach another Gospel of salvation are teaching demonic and antichrist doctrines. Even those doctrines that sound logical and reasonable and do not line up with God's Word are to be rejected. They are damaging to a Believer's walk with the Lord.

Our foundation is to be in Jesus Christ, and it is only through the Holy Spirit, as well as our unity in Love (Agape Love) in Him is the only way we can stand strong and not be moved by these false doctrines. This unity also includes knowing the scriptures, so that we may be able to stand against these lies with the Word of God. As previously shown in Chapter 3 Paul wrote to the Ephesians:

"[11] And His gifts were [varied; He Himself appointed and gave men to us] some to be apostles (special messengers), some prophets (inspired preachers and expounders), some evangelists (preachers of the Gospel, traveling missionaries), some pastors (shepherds of His flock) and teachers.

[12] His intention was the perfecting and the full equipping of the saints (His consecrated people), [that they should do] the work of ministering toward building up Christ's body (the church),

[13] [That it might develop] until we all attain oneness in the faith and in the comprehension of the [[b]full and accurate] knowledge of the Son of God, that [we might arrive] at really mature manhood (the completeness of personality which is nothing less than the standard height of Christ's own perfection), the measure of the stature of the fullness of the Christ and the completeness found in Him.

[14] So then, we may no longer be children, tossed [like ships] to and fro between chance gusts of teaching and wavering with every changing wind of doctrine, [the prey of] the cunning and cleverness of [c]unscrupulous men, [gamblers engaged] in every

shifting form of trickery in inventing errors to mislead." Ephesians 4:11-14 *(Amplified Bible)*

When Christians do not know the scripture or if they do not have Godly teachers that have been filled with the Holy Spirit and who do not teach sound doctrine; then the devil will find ways to infiltrate the church with false and damning heresies, in order that he may deceive and lead many astray. As long as he can distract us from keeping our eyes on Jesus; prevent us from reading the Word and from spending time alone with God; then he has succeeded. We must keep watch and not let ourselves be deceived.

Salvation is by No Other Name than the Name of Jesus

As already shown in the Foundational Truths found in Chapter 2, Jesus is the only way unto God. There are those who want to coddle the unsaved that come into their church through their "inclusiveness." Inclusiveness doesn't mean that we are to compromise the Gospel message of salvation. God doesn't wink at sin and neither should we. Instead "inclusiveness" means that we are to go out into the local neighborhood, to those on the streets, to those who are lost and most of all to those whom the Holy Spirit leads us and then to bring them into the church, so that they may know and hear about the love, power and mercy of God. Inclusiveness simply includes all that will hear.

The message of salvation offers love, acceptance and forgiveness; it is not to be confused with condoning a person's sin or sinful nature. Non-Christians are living in darkness and the Church is to be a shining city on a hill that shines into their darkness. Yet, when a church does not preach the Gospel or does not allow the Holy Spirit to move and convict sinners' hearts, then it no longer is fulfilling God's Divine Plan. It simply becomes a cold and dead religious gathering place. If the power, presence and love of Jesus aren't real in a church or in the lives of Christians in the church, then the church itself is lost and spiritually blind. How then can the blind and lost lead the blind and lost? It can't.

THE DIVINE MAGNET

John: 6:44 "No one is able to come to Me unless the Father Who sent Me attracts and draws him and gives him the desire to come to Me, and [then] I will raise him up [from the dead] at the last day." (Amplified Bible.)

"God is drawing you to Himself. This is not your own wish, and the stirring of your own heart, but the everlasting Divine magnet is drawing you. These restless yearnings and thirstings, remember, are the work of God. Come and be still, and wait upon God. He will reveal Himself."[20]

Oh how many times have we struggled to get close to God? How many times have we attempted to set aside time to pray or read the scriptures and ended up failing? And how often have we asked God to give us a greater desire to seek Him more? And how often have those prayers seemed to go unanswered?

God does not answer prayer when it comes to something that He has already completed or made a provision for. God wants us to know Him more than we want to know Him. He has made it possible for us to walk and talk with Him every day. He has also made it possible for us to be filled with His power and love, through Jesus Christ and by the Holy Spirit. Yet, how often do we either forget or fail to understand that it is not our own efforts that draw us closer to God? All too often we are relying upon the wrong things in our attempt to get close to God.

"You [we] are so occupied and filled with other things, religious things, preaching and praying, studying and working, so occupied with your[our] religion, that you [we] do not give God the time to make Himself known, and to enter in and to take possession."[21]

---

[20] Murray, Andrew (2009-10-04). The Master's Indwelling (p. 27). Public Domain Books. Kindle Edition.

[21] Ibid. (p. 27).

Oh how Andrew Murray is correct when he says it is "we" are so occupied doing things for God, that God is actually left standing on the sidelines. We feel that we've got to "save the world" for God; "write music" for God; "write books for God"; "preach for God"; and "reaching out to the poor and etc. for God". We make so many wonderful plans for God, build great churches and come up with great "Godly" ideas that we fail to take time to wait before God and find out what it really is that He has for us. We want and expect God to bless us and the things that we are doing without obtaining His direction first. Nowhere in scripture does it say that God blesses in this way.

"God created us that we might be the empty vessels in which He could work out His beauty, His will, His love, and the likeness of His blessed Son."[22]

"Empty Vessels", that is what we were created to be. We are to be Empty Vessels who wait patiently before Him, so that He can fill us with His Holy Spirit, Power, and Love. By being His Empty Vessels, we will then be able to fulfill His Will, because He will fill us to such an overflowing anointing, power and love that it will overflow to the world around us. In return, the world around us will see Jesus in us.

Yet we cannot be His Empty Vessel when we are filled with self, worldly things, worldly pleasures and ungodly desires. It is when we choose to come before Him, under the

---

[22] Murray, Andrew (2009-10-04). The Master's Indwelling (p. 26). Public Domain Books. Kindle Edition.

Holy Spirit's guidance and leading; and at Jesus feet empty out all the unholy things that are inside of us, through Christ's Precious, Cleansing Blood; it is only then will we experience and know God's Holiness residing fully inside of us. That is what the "everlasting Divine Magnet" is drawing us to do; so that we may become His Holy and Precious Vessels. Where God is, there is Holiness. Do you sense such a drawing and yearning?

"It is the most natural thing in creation that God should have me every moment, and that my God should be nearer to me than all else."[23]

"Moment by moment I'm kept in His love;
Moment by moment I've life from above;
Looking to Jesus till glory doth shine;
Moment by moment, O Lord, I am Thine."
(Daniel W. Whittle)

Our Heavenly Father who is Our "Divine Magnet", through His Son Jesus Christ, and by His Holy Spirit is drawing us constantly to Himself. He desires for us to know Him every moment of our life and to depend upon Him moment by moment. He sent Jesus to make the way possible and then He sent the Holy Spirit to lead us and fill our Empty

[23] Ibid. (p. 26).

Vessel every day with all the Fullness and Glory of the God Head. May we yield to Him moment by moment.

The Salvation Message Preached and Taught Under the Holy Spirit's Anointing

R.A. Torrey speaks about the difference that was made in his life and the life of others who were baptized with the Holy Spirit and power. He speaks about: "the wonderful experiences of Charles G. Finney, John Wesley, D. L. Moody and others. These men tell us that when they were baptized with the Holy Spirit they had wonderful sensations. Finney, for example, describes it as like great waves of electricity sweeping over him, so that he was compelled to ask God to withhold His hand, lest he die on the spot. Mr. Moody, on rare occasions, described a similar experience."[24]

It was because of their infilling of the Holy Spirit that these great men of God led thousands to Christ. Some had great revivals around the world. These men were praying men and they knew that they had to be renewed in the Holy Spirit every day. Through them the power of the Gospel message was preached.

---

[24] Torrey, R. A. (Reuben Archer) (2011-03-24). The Person and Work of The Holy Spirit (p. 136). . Kindle Edition.

Another example is T.L. and Daisy Osborn: when they began their ministry in the early 50's they failed miserably on their first mission trip to India. They came home defeated. T.L. wrote: "We returned home, profoundly disheartened, feeling we had failed. Within a few months, we experienced four visions that change the course of our lives."[25]

T.L. goes on to tell about their first encounter with the Lord after they heard Rev. Hattie Hammond preach, *"If You Ever See Jesus, You Can Never Be The Same Again."* After that they went home and Jesus appeared to T.L. the next morning and he stayed on his face praying until noon. Then he says that they "saw Jesus at work in a person;" via an anointed minister who preached and prayed for the sick, where many were healed and saved. They discovered Jesus in His Word and that "Whatever Jesus says He will do, we will expect Him to do it." The fourth vision came when they preached and prayed for the sick, everyone was healed and that they discovered Jesus at work in them.[26] For nearly 50 years, millions came to know Jesus and were healed under the anointed ministry of T.L. and Daisy. God's Divine Plan for the Church today is that millions upon millions come to know Jesus and receive healing and deliverance. Yet, unbelief and religion are hindering countless thousands of Christians and churches from fulfilling God's Divine Plan. What a tragedy.

---

[25] Osborn, T.L. (1997). The Message That Works. OSFO Publishers, Tulsa, OK.
[26] Ibid.

Another example is T.L. and Daisy Osborn when they began their ministry in the early 50's they failed miserably on their first missionary trip to India. They came home defeated. T.L. wrote, "We returned home, profoundly disheartened, feeling we had failed. Within a few months, we experienced revelations that change the course of our lives."

CHAPTER 6: THE HOLY SPIRIT AND REGENERATION

What is regeneration?

"Regeneration is the impartation of life, spiritual life, to those who are dead, spiritually dead, through their trespasses and sins (Eph. ii. 1, R. V.). It is the Holy Spirit who imparts this life."[27]

"To put the matter of regeneration in another way; regeneration is the impartation of a new nature, God's own nature to the one who is born again (2 Pet. i. 4)."[28]

Torrey goes on to explain that when we are born, we are born with a "perverted nature", and that we are "born blind to God's Truth." It doesn't matter about our background or upbringing, we seek to please ourselves. We lack the ability to understand Spiritual things. Only when we are born again, are we able to see "as God sees" and our spiritual nature then begins to line up with the same affections that God has. This is

---

[27] Torrey, R. A. (Reuben Archer) (2011-03-24). The Person and Work of The Holy Spirit (p. 59). . Kindle Edition.

[28] Ibid. (p. 60).

what the regenerating work of the Holy Spirit does in our life. Only the Holy Spirit can make us a "new creature."

Sudden Regeneration

"I believe in something far more wonderful than sudden conversion. I believe in sudden regeneration. Conversion is merely an outward thing, the turning around. Regeneration goes down to the deepest depths of the inmost soul, transforming thoughts, affections, will, the whole inward man. I believe in sudden regeneration because the Bible teaches it and because I have seen it times without number. I believe in sudden regeneration because I have experienced it."[29]

"If the religion of the future does not teach sudden miraculous conversion, if it does not teach something far more meaningful, sudden, miraculous regeneration by the power of the Holy Spirit, then the religion of the future will not be in conformity with the facts of experience and so will not be scientific. It will miss one of the most certain and most glorious of all truths."[30]

---

[29] Ibid. (p.61).
[30] Ibid. (p.61).

[31] Ibid. (pp. 61-62).

"Man-devised religions in the past have often missed the truth and man-devised religions in the future will doubtless do the same."[31][32]

In my life time, I have seen and met many people who have experienced "sudden regeneration." There was a man I met, when I was going to a Christian college, who had been a mob leader in Chicago. He told me how one day Jesus entered into his room and revealed Himself and called Him into the ministry. The Holy Spirit suddenly regenerated this man. He went from mobster to saint. I was amazed by his story, because I knew him as a kind and gentle man. Jesus still transforms lives today.

Paul writes about sudden regeneration in his letter to the Corinthian Church in 1 Corinthians 6:9-11:

> *"9 Do you not know that the unrighteous and the wrongdoers will not inherit or have any share in the kingdom of God? Do not be deceived (misled): neither the impure and immoral, nor idolaters, nor adulterers, nor those who participate in homosexuality,*
>
> *10 Nor cheats (swindlers and thieves), nor greedy graspers, nor drunkards, nor foulmouthed revilers and slanderers, nor extortioners and robbers*

---

[32] Ibid. (p.61).

will inherit or have any share in the kingdom of God.

¹¹ And such some of you were [once]. But you were washed clean (purified by a complete atonement for sin and made free from the guilt of sin), and you were consecrated (set apart, hallowed), and you were justified [pronounced righteous, by trusting] in the name of the Lord Jesus Christ and in the [Holy] Spirit of our God." (Amplified Bible)

How could wrongdoers, impure, immoral, idolaters, adulterers, those who participated in homosexuality, those who cheated, swindled, stole, those who were greedy, drunkards, foulmouthed, those who slandered, extorted others and who robbed others no longer live such lives? I had searched over and over for the "how" and it wasn't until I read Torrey's book, that the Holy Spirit pointed out to me that it was only by His regeneration power, that these individuals were purified, set free from their sinful lifestyles and made Holy in the name of Jesus and in the Holy Spirit. Why are so many churches overlooking this truth today? Why are they winking at sin and trying to coddle and be sympathetic to what the Holy Spirit and God's Word clearly defines as sinful and what will keep a person from entering into the Kingdom of God? I didn't say this, Torrey didn't say this; the Holy Spirit said this through Paul. The reason Churches and Christians are living defeated lives is because they have bought into the lie "that God didn't mean what He said." They have chosen to re-interpret or ignore what is plainly written. They are simply "Grieving the Holy Spirit." The Holy Spirit does not operate through those or a church that grieves Him. And they wonder why their church and Christian life is going nowhere.

The Difference between Regeneration and the Baptism with the Holy Spirit

"A man may be regenerated by the Holy Spirit and still not be baptized with the Holy Spirit. In regeneration, there is the impartation of life by the Spirit's power, and the one who receives it is saved: in the baptism with the Holy Spirit, there is the impartation of power, and the one who receives it is fitted for service. The baptism with the Holy Spirit, however, may take place at the moment of regeneration. It did, for example, in the household of Cornelius."[33]

Unfortunately, there are those who believe that when they receive Jesus Christ into their heart, that they are also "baptized with the Holy Spirit." Baptism with the Holy Spirit is a separate act. Simply study the Book of Acts and the evidence is there. Both salvation and Baptism with the Holy

---

[33] Torrey, R. A. (Reuben Archer) (2011-03-24). The Person and Work of The Holy Spirit (p. 101). . Kindle Edition.

Spirit happened at the same time at Cornelius house, because they believed what Peter was preaching about Jesus Christ. Torrey does a wonderful job explaining what the Baptism of the Holy Spirit is, in his book. When we are born anew, Jesus Christ enters into our life via the Holy Spirit. This is the regenerating work of the Holy Spirit. Jesus entering into our heart is not the baptism with the Holy Spirit. For further study on this matter, I highly recommend that you read Torrey's book for yourself. I could not possibly explain this in length the way he does. Yet, briefly I have included some of these insights in this book.

CHAPTER 7: LOVE ONE ANOTHER

"³⁴ A new commandment I give unto you, That ye love one another; as I have loved you, that ye also love one another.

³⁵ By this shall all men know that ye are my disciples, if ye have love one to another." John 13:

Jesus Commanded Love for One Another

"Love one another" is found 20 times in the New Testament. Jesus said it four times in the Book of John alone and He also made it a commandment.³⁴ Jesus made it clear, "by this [the world] will know that you are my disciples." We can either prove to the world that we love one another, or we can continue to argue, judge and condemn one another and prove to the world that we are no different than they. Yet, this love does not always come easy for us. In reality, it is humanly impossible for us to love in this manner on our own. This love <u>Jesus is talking about is</u> "Divine" "Agape" love. Dick Mills,

---

³⁴ John 13:24-35; and Colossians 3:12-17

who was a Great Evangelist and Greek Scholar, wrote this about Agape:

"God's AGAPE love gives and gives, then keeps on giving, never really asking for anything in exchange. AGAPE is a beautiful concept, a love not based on emotions or feelings. It is actually a love by choice, a love that doesn't look for an affinity. AGAPE gives us the ability to love that which is unlovely."[35]

Dick says this type of love"

A. Is "a love by choice;"

B. It "gives and gives;"

C. It "keeps on giving;"

D. It never asks "for anything in exchange;"

E. It is not "based on emotions or feelings;"

F. It doesn't "look for affinity", which means it doesn't rely upon a spontaneous or natural liking or attraction for someone or have another person spontaneously love us or show any natural liking or attraction for us.[36] And;

G. It has "the ability to love that which is unlovely."

This love comes from the Father and can only be shed abroad in our hearts by the Holy Spirit. It was impossible for the Disciples and those in the Upper Room to love in this manner until they received the "Gift of the Holy Spirit" (until they were baptized with the Holy Spirit). Without the Holy

---

[35] Mills, Dick, "The 4 Loves", https://www.smashwords.com/books/view/235173/
[36] Google Search

Spirit, it is impossible for us to love as Jesus commanded. Jesus desires to love others through us. He has not commanded us to love others on our own.

The Conditional Promise

"15 If ye love me, keep my commandments."

"21 He that hath my commandments, and keepeth them, he it is that loveth me: and he that loveth me shall be loved of my Father, and I will love him, and will manifest myself to him."

"23 Jesus answered and said unto him, If a man love me, he will keep my words: and my Father will love him, and we will come unto him, and make our abode with him." John 14

Jesus gives us the command to love with Agape love. Then He adds a conditional promise to His command, that when we do love with Agape love:

A. It will be proof of our Love for Him;

B. In return the Father and He will love us and manifest Themselves to us;

C. He and the Father then will come and make Their "Home and dwelling place" inside of us.

Only through the Holy Spirit are we able to do this.

The Church is to have the Divine Agape Love Flowing through It at All Times

While there are those in the Church who speak of God's love and quote 1 Corinthians 13, there seems to be so few who actually live it and demonstrate it. We know that this is what we are supposed to do, yet we fail so many times in keeping our Lord's command to Love one another. Why? Could it be because we have not earnestly desired this Love, nor have we truly sought after it? Perhaps we have "choked" it out with the cares of the world? This Love can only shed abroad in our hearts by the Holy Spirit. And as already mentioned, we can only know this Agape love when we receive the gift of the Holy Spirit (i.e. are baptized with the Holy Spirit.) It comes no other way.

We are to Demonstrate Brotherly Love towards One Another

"Be kindly affectioned one to another with brotherly love; in honour preferring one another;" Romans 12:10

Paul here uses the word "Philadelphia" which comes from the root word PHILEO. Dick Mills says that: "PHILEO is a word that has to do with feelings for people."[37] It also means an "affection or feeling towards" someone. In his first letter to the Church in Thessalonica, Paul uses both "Philadelphia" and

"AGAPAN" (from the word AGAPE), which shows us that along with Divine Love, we are to have Brotherly Love, which again comes from the Love of God shed abroad in our hearts by the Holy Spirit.

> *"But as touching brotherly love ye need not that I write unto you: for ye yourselves are taught of God to love one another." 1 Thessalonians 4:9*

Peter also uses the word "Philadelphia" and "Philadelphos", which means to be friendly:

> *"Finally, be ye all of one mind, having compassion one of another, love as brethren, be pitiful, be courteous:" 1 Peter 3:8.*

Therefore, not only AGAPE Love is to flow through us, but also PHILADELPHIA Love for our brothers and sisters in Christ. Without being surrendered to the Holy Spirit, it is not possible for either one of these loves to flow through us as they should. Our human efforts to love are not enough.

Human Attributes are not Enough

We can be the most kind, compassionate and generous Christian on this planet and yet not have Agape Love. God has

[37] Dick Mills. The 4 Loves (Kindle Locations 167-168).

chosen to give us this love, yet have we chosen to receive it? Just as Jesus promised that the Father would baptize those who ask with the Holy Spirit, so too will the Father shed His Love abroad in our hearts when we are baptized with the Holy Spirit. (More about this will be discussed herein.) I have a simple Biblical philosophy, "No ask – No receive" and "No believe – No Receive." We don't have Agape Love shed abroad in our hearts because we either have never asked to baptized with the Holy Spirit or we simply don't believe that God's promises are for us and/or we have choked it out with the cares of this world. Ask and you shall receive.

Spiritual Pride is Hate and not Love

I have found that the greatest downfall in many churches and in Christians' lives is Spiritual Pride. Pride in and of itself is "the mother of all sin", and I believe that Spiritual Pride is a demonic destructive force that negates the very meaning of the word Christian and it opens up the gates of hell to freely destroy not only the one bound by Spiritual Pride, but also those they lash out at in judgment and condemnation. Normally, Spiritual Pride is used to elevate oneself or one's church above other Christians and other churches. Neither God nor the Holy Spirit will have anything to do with Spiritual Pride. It comes straight from hell.

The Opposite of Love is Indifference

Unfortunately Religion also brings about indifference towards those that don't follow a certain religious way. Indifference is the cruelest form of hate. It is an outright refusal to let God's love through the Holy Spirit to flow through our heart for another person. Indifference is a refusal to obey our Lord's command to forgive or to pray for or to do good to our enemies. Indifference is worse than murder, because it numbs our heart and conscience to the point where we don't care whether or not a person lives or dies. God sent Jesus into the world so that man would not perish without Him.[38] Indifference cares nothing about God's love for a person. Indifference prevents the Holy Spirit and God from operating in our life. The devil and his demons are indifferent to us and wish to destroy us and separate us from God for all eternity. Indifference is actually joining forces with Satan for the downfall and destruction of another. Indifference must be quickly repented of and God's mercy, love and forgiveness sought. [39] When we are deliberately indifferent, we shut out the Holy Spirit. This not only grieves the Holy Spirit, but puts us on the edge of blasphemy, which we know is an "unforgivable sin." It is only through the Holy Spirit, with the confession of our sinful indifference and our repentance of it that allows the Blood of Christ to cleanse us from this sin. We

[38] John 3:16
[39] Psalm 51

must not hesitate in separating ourselves from indifference. (1 John 1:9).

To Be Like Jesus is More Than Words

I like giving this example:

Mahatma Gandhi was once asked what he had against Jesus. He replied, "... I don't reject Christ. I love Christ. It's just that so many of you Christians are so unlike Christ. If Christians would really live according to the teachings of Christ, as found in the Bible, all of India would be Christian today." [40]

The Love of God Shed Abroad In Our Hearts

"And hope maketh not ashamed; because the love of God is shed abroad in our hearts by the Holy Ghost which is given unto us". Romans 5:5

Without the Love of God shed abroad in our hearts by the Holy Spirit[41] it is truly impossible for us to love one another as our Lord has commanded. Sure we can love those we like, and we can even show love towards others in our church, but our Lord's command applies to all Believers in the Body of Christ, whether or not we agree with their doctrines or like the church that they attend. God didn't leave it up to us to

---

[40] www.thinkexist.com
[41] Romans 5:5

pick and choose whom to love and whom not to love. Why did He love us and why does He still love us? We can forget this so easily, and when we do, we often end up judging or even gossiping about someone, which opens the demonic door to Spiritual Pride or Indifference. The only way we can be assured that we have God's love in our heart is to daily confess that without the Lord and without the Holy Spirit we are weak, and ask the Father to continue to shed His love for others abroad in our heart. He will answer such a prayer.

CHAPTER 8: GO UNDER THE HOLY SPIRIT'S POWER AND ANOINTING AND MAKE DISCIPLES

"Go ye therefore, and make disciples of all the nations, baptizing them into the name of the Father and of the Son and of the Holy Spirit:" Matthew 28:19(ASV)

"³ To whom also he shewed himself alive after his passion by many infallible proofs, being seen of them forty days, and speaking of the things pertaining to the kingdom of God:

⁴ And, being assembled together with them, commanded them that they should not depart from Jerusalem, but wait for the promise of the Father, which, saith he, ye have heard of me.

⁸ But ye shall receive power, after that the Holy Ghost is come upon you: and ye shall be witnesses unto me

both in Jerusalem, and in all Judaea, and in Samaria,
and unto the uttermost part of the earth."Acts1:3-5

The Disciples were told to Wait until They Received Power

All though the disciples had been with Jesus at least three years and twice they had experienced preaching the Kingdom of God, healing the sick and casting out devils; they were not allowed to go out and make disciples or do anything that they had done before, until the Holy Spirit was outpoured upon them. And when the Holy Spirit came, they were all baptized with Holy Spirit. After which, Peter rose up to speak and under the Holy Spirit's anointing He preached Jesus Christ crucified, which led to at least 3,000 to repentance, being baptized with water and then receiving the baptism with the Holy Spirit, in the same manner as those upon whom He first fell in the Upper Room. The Greek root word for this Divine power is "dunamos." We get the word "dynamite" from it.

Jesus knew that they could do nothing without Him and the Holy Spirit's power. When they were baptized with the Holy Spirit, Jesus entered into their lives. They now had a new boldness and Divine power. And as we read in Acts and in the following epistles and letters, we are able to see that it was with this power and anointing that there were able to preach the Gospel, with signs, wonders and miracles following, and as a result the Church rapidly grew. Without the Holy Spirit and His power, the Church would have never come into existence. Yet there are churches that try to make disciples without the Holy Spirit and His power. God's Plan does not include powerless disciples

The Command to "Go" is for the Church and those in Christ

In Matthew 28:18-20 and Mark 16:15-16, Jesus gives the command to go into all nations, to teach and preach the Gospel to everyone. As shown in the verse above, the American Standard Version in Matthew 28:19 says to go and "make disciples". When the Holy Spirit was outpoured on the Day of Pentecost, the Apostles were finally able to fulfill this command.[42] This command was a command for the whole Church. Whether or not we are called into the ministry, we are still under that command to be living witnesses and to make disciples. We can do this by living a Holy Life and being filled with the Holy Spirit. Jesus Christ should be so evident in our life that even when we are confronted with persecution, verbal abuse, attacks and every negative thing, the Love of God in our heart will triumph over all things that we encounter.[43] Our

---

[42] Acts 1:4-8

personal life should reflect Christ so much so that people cannot help but ask why we are so different, which will give us an open door to witness.[44] Such a personal relationship with the Lord will also allow us to be sensitive to the Holy Spirit's prompting and leading. When our relationship with the Lord is close, the Holy Spirit will speak to us and let us know when it is the right moment for us to reach out to help someone or to speak to someone in need.   These are what I can divine appointments.

Witnessing

Witnessing under the Holy Spirit's leading and anointing is the only true way to witness to someone. Torrey and Murray both speak about being surrendered to the Holy Spirit's leading every minute of our life. Such leading, keeps us from error and opens the door for us to witness to the right person or persons who are ready to hear. There are those who believe that they must "save the world" or "save their community." We can save no one. Only the Holy Spirit can convict a person's heart and reveal Jesus Christ to someone. He will do it through us if we will let Him.

I can remember in my high school years, that there was a tract that said. "4 Thing God Wants You to Know." There

---

[43] Colossians 1:9-12; and I Corinthians 13
[44] Colossians 2:6-10

were Christians who were trained on how to present this tract and convince people that they needed Jesus Christ. These people were also taught to witness to everyone they met. However, not everyone we meet is ready to listen to the Gospel message. "God Compels No Man to Serve Him." Torrey says: "It is manifestly not God's intention that we speak to every one we meet."[45] Again, this is where discernment comes in. It is far better to be witnessing to someone who is ready to listen. Only the Holy Spirit can direct us to the right person. And when we encounter those with hardened hearts, we still should be living witnesses in their presence. Jesus is to be living in us and through us at all times.

Words vs. Actions

"And they overcame him by the blood of the Lamb, and by the word of their testimony; and they loved not their lives unto the death." Rev. 12:11

There is this unscriptural belief that says, "It is better to be silent and let people see that you are a Christian than to tell others about Jesus Christ!" Where this lie originated from I don't know? How can we feed and clothe others and not tell them about Jesus? What good is it that we just feed or warm

---

[45] Torrey, R. A. (Reuben Archer) (2011-03-24). The Person and Work of The Holy Spirit (p. 92). . Kindle Edition.

their body, when their soul is bound for hell? The world around us is dying. They need Jesus just as much as we do.

The truth is that those who are filled with the Holy Spirit, who walk in the Spirit and who are led by the Spirit do not remain silent. There is an overflowing love and joy in them that they can't contain. Sure, in a work place or family situation or among those that would kill us if we witnessed, our actions can be our testimony of the One Who dwells within. Still, we should never pass up a divine opportunity that the Holy Spirit gives us to witness. Salvation does not come by osmosis.

Jesus did not say, "Go out into the world and live good Christian lives in hope that some may turn from their wicked ways and come unto Me." This was not His command. If the disciples had been silent and the early Christians had been silent, there'd be no Church today!

When we meet people, especially those we may never see again, we must be sensitive to the Holy Spirit. There will be times when the door is open for us to speak the Words that the Holy Spirit has put in our heart, in order to lead that person to Christ, or to at least sow a seed. This also applies to helping those in need. Oh may the Holy Spirit convict our hearts so much so, that we repent of our excuses as to why we aren't living witnesses of Jesus Christ. May the world around us truly know that we are Christians by the word of our testimony. May they know we belong to Him by our love.

Spreading the Good News

"But we preach Christ crucified, unto the Jews a stumbling block, and unto the Greeks foolishness;" 1 Corinthians 1:23

The Gospel or "Good News" is that Jesus not only died for our sins, but He also bore our sicknesses and diseases and we don't have to bare them.[46] The "Good News" also includes the fact that Jesus came to Earth to make us Holy,[47] so that a Holy God and Jesus could dwell within us by His Holy Spirit.[48] People need to know and be taught that God desires to communicate and fellowship with them. That He desires to bestow "good and perfect gifts" upon them[49], which we call blessings. He also desires for them to live with Him for all eternity in a place called Heaven, where there is no more death, no more sickness, sorrow, pain or suffering. Everyone needs to hear and know that God is a caring and loving God and that He is concerned about the very minutest detail of our

---

[46] Isaiah 53:5-6; 1 Peter 2:4
[47] 2 Timothy 1:9
[48] John 14:17; Romans 8:9; 1 Corinthians 3:16; and Ephesians 3:17
[49] James 1:17

lives.[50] God has only good and prosperity in mind for us.[51] All need to know that Jesus is interceding constantly for everyone that belongs to God.[52] These are just the highlights of what the Gospel message is all about.

Speak as God's Oracle under the Holy Spirit's Anointing

*"If any man speak, let him speak as the **oracle**s of God; if any man minister, let him do it as of the ability which God giveth: that God in all things may be glorified through Jesus Christ, to whom be praise and dominion for ever and ever. Amen." 1 Peter 4:11*

Oh how it grieves my heart when a pastor or preacher orates and says little or nothing about the Gospel message. I can't help but wonder if it does not also grieve the Holy Spirit, because He is not freely allowed to speak through or minister through that pastor or preacher? Why have so many found it more thrilling to give great orations and lack the desire to be true "oracles of God?" Why do so many churches leave no room for the Holy Spirit to move or to speak? On the other hand, why are there those who believe that they must drum up the Holy Spirit's moving or beg and plead for Him to move in the way that they want Him to and not the way God desires?

---

[50] Matthew 6
[51] Jeremiah 29:11-12
[52] Romans 8:24; and Hebrews 7:25

How can one truly preach or teach the Gospel without the Holy Spirit? Yes, many have great scriptural knowledge and have been well trained in seminaries on how to present a sermon, but what good is it if God, by His Holy Spirit has no part in the preparation? Is the Gospel Message that boring or no longer relevant today? Without the Holy Spirit the Gospel message cannot be fully preached.

Making Disciples is a One-on-One Ministry

Making disciples should be a one-on-one event. True, churches have "discipleship" classes, but usually they are not the same as personally mentoring a new Believer. In general, it is often hard for a person to confide their personal fears, questions, doubts and anxieties in a group. As to where, when a person has someone he or she can speak to without fear, knowing that no matter what they will be loved and accepted, it makes it easier to disciple them. A true discipleship class should train people how to be one-on-one disciples. If the church wants to teach others about church doctrine or about the Bible, then the class should be entitled something else. I recently read in a discipleship study that 70% who come to Christ fall away after 2 years, because they had no one to disciple them. The Church needs more one-on-one disciples; disciples that can be trusted; disciples that have the love of God in their heart; disciples that are filled with the power of the Holy Spirit; disciples that have patience and will give encouragement and take time to meet with and pray with the new Believer. This is what Jesus had in mind when He said "Go and make disciples..."

Being Like Jesus Requires Doing the Father's Will

Many say they want to be like Jesus, but not all follow in His footsteps. He came to do the Will of the Father, and the Words that He spoke were the Words that the Father gave Him.[53] And how did He receive these Words of Life? He received them through the Holy Spirit. We read in Acts and throughout the Epistles that the Apostles spoke under the anointing and leading of Holy Spirit and how they preached the Gospel message with power and not with man's wisdom.[54] And when they preached the Gospel, God manifested Himself with signs, wonders and miracles following. They never got tired of preaching "Jesus Christ crucified." They never got tired of preaching and teaching the Good News of salvation, healing, deliverance and hope. Jesus did it and so did all those who followed Him. The Holy Spirit was given so that we may have God's power to be living witnesses to a dying world. Yet, there are those who shun the Holy Spirit and His power and rely upon self and self-obtained knowledge and wisdom to preach the Gospel. If they truly knew the Lord they would seek

---

[53] 1 John 5:20; and John 14:10
[54] 1 Corinthians 1:18; 2:4; 4:20; and 1 Thessalonians 1:5

Him more and more each day, and they would be renewed daily in their hearts and minds by the Holy Spirit. May we never be found guilty of shutting out the Holy Spirit in our life!

CHAPTER 9: DIVINE HEALING

God's Plan for Healing and Wholeness has Never Changed!

Healing comes in many different forms and ways. There are the kind words that heal a broken spirit. There is the gentle caring touch that heals and uplifts. There is laughter that heals when we are down. There is the warm embrace that heals loneliness, sadness and sorrow. There is healing that comes from friends who choose to stand with us no matter what. There is healing in love. There is healing in forgiveness. Healing comes from acceptance. Good news brings healing to the heart. Encouraging words bring healing and uplift to our mind and spirit. Healing comes from answered prayer. Healing comes in so many unexpected ways and even from a stranger's kindness. Yet more than this, healing that brings the wholeness we need comes from God Himself. He is the great healer.

The Church is to be a Healing Place

The Early Church became a place where people could come for Spiritual, mental and physical healing. They followed our Lord's example by ministering to the whole person. There were "Love Feasts"[55], where Christians assembled, ate together, worshipped together, prayed together and one for another. The Early Church was a place where healing was common place. The Church is still called to be the same healing place today. As we know, many churches and Christian faiths do not heed this calling. Why is this so?

No Believe, No Receive

I researched for nearly a year to find out why the Church became more formal and relied less on the Holy Spirit. I found that after John the beloved died, a cessationalist doctrine began to rapidly infiltrate the Church. Cessationalism is the belief that after the last apostle died the gifts of the Holy Spirit died with him and therefore they were no longer needed, and that included Divine Healing. Those who believed this and still do today are called cessationalists. Another word for this doctrine is called "unbelief." It makes me want to ask these people, "When did God stop being God?"

God brings healing to our mind, soul and body. He offers healing to the whole person.

Man's religious philosophies, doctrines, teachings and so forth have rationalized the Biblical truth about healing.

---

[55] Jude 1:12

They have either, side-stepped the issue, or said it no longer exists and/or it is limited to certain circumstances and methods; all of which negate what the Bible says. As a result, millions over the years have been encapsulated into believing these lies and have missed out on many wonderful blessings that God provides. In other words, just like in the Garden of Eden when the serpent told Eve that God didn't mean what He said, so these religious men have bought into and sold the same lie to their denominations, churches and followers. And even today, they keep millions from experiencing God's miraculous healing power. Yes, God still heals!

From all the teachings I have read by Orthodox and non-Orthodox Christian writers, the majority agree that when God created Adam and Eve, He planned for them to be healthy and whole for all eternity. When they listened to the serpent and ate from the tree of "Knowledge of Good and Evil", sin entered into the world and with sin, eventually death, sickness and disease would soon follow. God didn't punish them because they disobeyed his command not to eat from that tree; instead it was their choice that brought all of this upon them. They gave up their healthy life with God to the devil's destructive control. God however, didn't withdraw His plan for health and wholeness; throughout the Old Testament we read about Him healing and declaring Himself as "the One who Heals." We also read in both the Old and New Testament that Jesus, the Son of God would not only pay the penalty for mankind's sins, but that He would also pay the price for mankind's healing.

All Healing Comes in the Name of Jesus and through the Holy Spirit

"How God anointed Jesus of Nazareth with the Holy Ghost and with power: who went about doing good, and healing all that were oppressed of the devil; for God was with him." Acts 10:38

"Now Peter and John went up together into the temple at the hour of prayer, being the ninth hour.

2 And a certain man lame from his mother's womb was carried, whom they laid daily at the gate of the temple which is called Beautiful, to ask alms of them that entered into the temple;

3 Who seeing Peter and John about to go into the temple asked an alms.

4 And Peter, fastening his eyes upon him with John, said, Look on us.

5 And he gave heed unto them, expecting to receive something of them.

⁶ Then Peter said, Silver and gold have I none; but such as I have give I thee: In the name of Jesus Christ of Nazareth rise up and walk.

⁷ And he took him by the right hand, and lifted him up: and immediately his feet and ankle bones received strength.

⁸ And he leaping up stood, and walked, and entered with them into the temple, walking, and leaping, and praising God." Acts 3:1-8

Throughout the book of Acts we see the apostles full of the Holy Spirit healing people everywhere they went. We also read about healing, signs wonders and miracles taking place throughout the rest of the New Testament. We see in James that the Church is to be a place where people come for healing. God remains in the Healing business today.

The Gifts of Healings

"To another faith by the same Spirit; to another the gifts of healing by the same Spirit; I Corinthians 12: 9

"And God hath set some in the church, first apostles, secondarily prophets, thirdly teachers, after that

miracles, then gifts of healings, helps, governments, diversities of tongues." 1 Corinthians 12:28"

All healing comes from God, in the name of Jesus, and through the Holy Spirit. The Holy Spirit is not limited in the way He heals. As I stated in the first paragraph of this chapter, healing comes in many different forms and ways. Healing can be miraculous or it can be gradual. It can happen in a church, an evangelistic meeting, on the mission field, among two or more people praying and healing can take place when we pray to God and ask Him to heal us. The Holy Spirit operates in different ways.

Personal Experiences Involving the Gifts of Healings

There is no one on this Earth that can convince me that God doesn't heal. I have not only seen Him heal over and over again, but I also have been healed many times. When I was a freshman at ORU, I had the privilege of praying for people to receive the Baptism with the Holy Spirit. I had never done this before. I can remember this large Swedish man from Minnesota, wanting to receive the infilling of the Holy Spirit. At first, I laid hands on him and prayed and I could see him struggling trying to receive the Holy Spirit. So I stopped and said to him, that I was going to simply lay my hands on his head and only say the name of "Jesus" and at the moment I told him just believe Jesus will baptize you. He was kneeling at a chair; I laid my hand on him and said, "Jesus!" It was like a lightning bolt had gone through me and I jumped and he jumped as if he had been shocked and suddenly he was praising God in an unknown language. After a minute or so he stopped. I asked him why he had stopped. With tears running down his cheeks, he said that he had been in a car accident two years earlier and could never raise his hands above his shoulders. Now he was raising them above his head. God had not only healed him but also baptized him with the Holy Spirit! Praise God.

The second miraculous experience was about a year later. I had flown out to California, from Tulsa, to be at Oral Robert's last public crusade which was being held in Pasadena. After he had preached, and before he began praying for those who needed healing, he would always go back stage and pray for the invalid and those who couldn't make it through the prayer line. Along with Oral, many ministers, some ORU students, his son Richard and I, we took turns praying for people and God was healing every one of them. At the end of the row of chairs, there sat a man with his three year old daughter on his lap. He said that she had muscular dystrophy and had never been able to stand or walk on her own. Oral backed off and told Richard and I to pray for her. As we did, I felt the love and compassion of Jesus that He had for little children. At the same time, Richard and I lifted her off her father's lap and stood her on the floor. With tears streaming down our faces we watched God heal and strengthen that little girl's legs. Man, there wasn't a dry eye in that place. If I had never encountered another healing miracle in my life, this alone would have been enough proof that Jesus heals. Yes, the Holy Spirit was manifesting Himself that day with the gift of healing. And He still does the same today.

Examples of Healing in the Old Testament:

God Answers Abraham's Prayer

The first healing example is found in Genesis Chapter 20. Abraham and his wife Sarah on their journey to the Promise Land stopped in the Land of Gerar. Abraham fearing that they might kill him and take away his lovely wife; told her to pretend to be his sister. Gerar's king Abimelech greeted them and asked if Sarah was his wife, and Abraham said she was his sister. (Actually Sarah was his half-sister.) So the king took Sarah into his tent for the night, but he didn't touch her. However, an angel of God appeared to him in a dream warning him not to touch her.

Abimelech was quite upset with Abraham and questioned him as to why he had lied to him and Abraham explained that his lie was based on his fear. But another thing had happened, because Abimelech had taken Sarah in; all the women's wombs in Gerar had "dried up".

> *"So Abraham prayed unto God: and God healed Abimelech, and his wife, and his maidservants; and they bare children." (Genesis 20:16-18).* God answered Abraham's prayer for healing.

God Declares Himself as the Healer

When the Children of Israel were in the desert following Moses, God gave them a conditional promise and announced Himself as their Healer.

> *"And said, If thou wilt diligently hearken to the voice of the LORD thy God, and wilt do that which is right in his sight, and wilt give ear to his commandments, and keep all his statutes, I will put none of these diseases upon thee, which I have brought upon the Egyptians: for I am the LORD that healeth thee."(Exodus 15:25-27).*

God Answers Moses' Prayers for Healing

Moses' sister, Miriam along with their brother Aaron, opposed Moses' marriage to a Cushite woman. As a result she was smitten with leprosy. Moses prayed to God, and God healed her.[56] Later on the children of Israel complained against the Lord and the Lord sent fiery serpents, which bit

---

[56] Numbers 12:1-16; and Deuteronomy 24:9

them and many died. They pleaded to Moses' to intercede for them and He prayed to the Lord that He would heal them. God told Moses to make a serpent of brass and put it on a pole, and whoever looked upon it would be healed.[57] The Church has always held that the "brazen serpent on the pole" represented Jesus Christ in the future being raised on the cross for our healing and salvation.

Healing Miracles under Elisha

In Second Kings Chapter 2, we read that when Elijah the Prophet was taken up to heaven; his mantle fell down on the ground for Elisha. This mantle was anointed by God's Spirit. Elisha went into Jericho and while he was there he was told that the water was killing everything around it. So Elisha poured salt into the water and Elisha revealed that it was the Lord who healed the waters.[58] We also read that God restored the life of the widow's son, with whom Elisha had stayed with from time to time.[59] Also through Elisha God healed King Naaman's leprosy.[60]

God Hears the Prayers of Hezekiah

Hezekiah took reign over Israel and Judah in Jerusalem at a young age. The priests under him found the books of the law, which had been ignored by his predecessors. Hezekiah

---

[57] Numbers 21:5-9
[58] 2 Kings 2:20-22
[59] 2 Kings 4:8-37
[60] 2 Kings 5:1-19

called for the nation to gather together to hear the reading of the law. Those that refused to come; God's fierce wrath was poured out against them. Hezekiah prayed to the Lord to forgive them and heal them. God granted His request.[61]

According to 2 Kings 20, King Hezekiah was extremely ill and was about to die. God had already delivered him and Jerusalem from Sennacherib's mighty Assyrian army. During that time Hezekiah learned how to pray and plead his cause unto the Lord. The Lord heard him and told the Prophet Isaiah that the Assyrians would be turned back (read Chapters 18-19). Now here lays Hezekiah about to die. So he turned his face to the wall and pleads his cause to the Lord. The Lord answered him through Isaiah and told Hezekiah that he would heal him in three days and grant him 15 more years to live. This proves that God is a compassionate healing God.

David Claims that God Heals; He is Our Health, and Heals All Our Diseases

"O LORD my God, I cried unto thee, and thou hast healed me." (Psalms30:2).

"Why art thou cast down, O my soul? and why art thou disquieted within me? Hope thou in God: for I shall yet praise him, who is the health of my

---

[61] 2 Chronicles 20:30

countenance, and my God." (Psalm 42:11).

"Who forgiveth all thine iniquities; who healeth all thy diseases;" (Psalm 103:3)

Jesus Christ is revealed in the Old Testament as the One who paid the price for our sins, sicknesses and diseases

"But he was wounded for our transgressions, he was bruised for our iniquities: the chastisement of our peace was upon him; and with his stripes we are healed."(Isaiah 53:5)

Saint Peter Confirms this in the New Testament

"Who his own self bare our sins in his own body on the tree, that we, being dead to sins, should live unto righteousness: by whose stripes ye were healed." 1 Peter 2:4

Miracles and Healing took place in the Old Testament period. Jesus came and proved that it was His Father's Will to keep on healing and under the Holy Spirit's anointing, His disciples continued on with God's desire for miracles and healing in a greater way. Does not the scripture say that God does not change, and does it not also say that "Jesus Christ the

same, yesterday, today and forever?"[62]   The Holy Spirit is
God's Spirit and is inseparable from God.   Just because
unbelieving men have taken scripture and twisted it, doesn't
mean that God is no longer God, nor His power has
diminished.   What a terrible lie has been delivered to the
Church over the centuries.   The Good News is that not
everyone has believed this lie.

The Good News is that Jesus Bore Our Sicknesses and Diseases

The Gospel or "Good News" is that Jesus not only died
for our sins, but He also bore our sicknesses and diseases and
we don't have to bare them. Both the Old and New Testament
speak about our Lord taking our sin and sicknesses upon Him.
It is "by His stripes we were healed." The word "healed" is a
completed task. Many struggle with this because they have
not been properly taught or they do not believe divine healing
is for them. Jesus came to do the Father's Will and that
included healing "all that were sick and oppressed by the
devil." The Church is called to pray for the sick.

> *"14 Is any sick among you? let him call for the elders*
> *of the church; and let them pray over him, anointing*
> *him with oil in the name of the Lord:*

---

[62] Hebrews 13:8

[15] And the prayer of faith shall save the sick, and the Lord shall raise him up; and if he have committed sins, they shall be forgiven him.

[16] Confess your faults one to another, and pray one for another, that ye may be healed. The effectual fervent prayer of a righteous man availeth much."
James 5

The Gifts of Healings Belong to the Local Church

Here are plain simple instructions for the Church that include forgiveness, (salvation), and healing. Let's take a closer look at these instructions. When there are sick people in the Church, they are to call for the Spiritual leaders, who are to pray the prayer of faith, through the Holy Spirit, over them, anointing them with oil in Jesus Name, and as a result the Lord will heal them. Still there is more to this.

The Prayer of Faith Brings Healing

"But without faith it is impossible to please him: for he that cometh to God must believe that he is, and that he is a rewarder of them that diligently seek him." Hebrews 11:6

The prayer of faith is required. Faith requires that those praying for the sick person not only know God's scriptural promises of healing, but that they also believe God will heal that person. It is not up to them to question or doubt whether or not God will heal, it is simply required that they have faith, full assurance, a full belief that God will heal. The Holy Spirit is the One Who prays the prayer of faith through the leaders.

God Brings Healing Through the Prayers of the Righteous

The Elders are to be righteous and so is everyone in Jesus Christ. Jesus Christ is our righteousness. He must fully live in our hearts via the Holy Spirit. A righteous person is someone full of the Holy Spirit and who seeks God with their whole being. Further, they continually intercede for others through the Holy Spirit praying for them. They seek God diligently with the faith that He will reward their prayers. Their prayers are led and anointed by the Holy Spirit and God hears and answers them, because the Holy Spirit prays the Will of God. Through the Righteousness of Christ we have an assuring faith. When a Righteous person prays for someone's healing, they will pray under the Holy Spirit's anointing and leading,. They have faith that God will answer.

Confession Brings Healing

Confessing our faults one to another and praying for one another is a very serious matter that will bring about healing. We simply can't confess our faults just to anyone. Unfortunately, there are pastors and Christians who cannot be confided in. We must seek out those who will not only keep what we say secret, but who also will love and accept us no matter what. And we in return must do the same.

God Desires to both Heal and Forgive

Confession and forgiveness are connected to divine healing. It is true that God heals those who don't come to Him for salvation, and it is also true that many are saved but never seek healing from God. This is where the Gospel message comes in and is to be preached and taught that God saves and heals the whole person. Just because a church has not done this before or it is not their practice, is not a justifiable excuse not to obey the Scriptures. A church that is submitted to the Holy Spirit will be a church that sees many saved and many miracles taking place as they did in the Early Church. What a glorious thought.

CHAPTER 10: PRAYER AND INTERCESSORY PRAYER

"Christ actually meant prayer to be the great power by which His Church should do its work, and that the neglect of prayer is the great reason the Church has not greater power over the masses in Christian and in heathen countries."[63]

"The power of the Church truly to bless rests on intercession—asking and receiving heavenly gifts to carry to men. Because this is so, it is no wonder that where, owing to lack of teaching or spiritual insight, we trust in our own diligence and effort, to the influence of the world and the flesh, and work more than we pray, the presence and power of God are not seen in our work as we would wish."[64]

---

[63] Murray, Andrew (2009-10-04). The Ministry of Intercession A Plea for More Prayer (p. 4). Public Domain Books. Kindle Edition.

[64] Ibid, (p. 5-6)

Intercessory Prayer is the Most Powerful Weapon

The most powerful weapon the Church has is intercessory prayer. This weapon is to be used continually from the Spiritual hierarchy down to the lay person. Christians everywhere should be taught how to rely upon the Holy Spirit to teach them how to pray effectively and unceasingly. Intercessory prayer not only changes the person praying but also has a mighty effect upon those being prayed for. Without the Holy Spirit praying through us, we cannot pray effectively.

> *"...The effectual fervent prayer of a righteous man availeth much.." James 5:16*

Only with the Holy Spirit, can we pray effectively and fervently. And when we pray in the Spirit, God hears us and answers, because the Holy Spirit knows how to pray and what to pray. Therefore, for our prayer life and intercessory prayer life to be effective, we must rely upon the Holy Spirit to lead us in prayer. Through the Holy Spirit, prayer becomes most powerful.

It was Through Prayer and the Holy Spirit that the Early Church Saw Victory

Torrey points out that "under the inspiration of the Holy

Spirit" the Early Church experienced "constant victory" and "perpetual progress."[65] He also states that through the entire Book of Acts shows that: "in those days there was a revival all the time and accessions every day of those who not only "hit the trail" but "were [really] being saved."[66]

Torrey shows the reason for this:

"And they continued stedfastly in the apostles' doctrine and fellowship, and in breaking of bread, and in prayers." Acts 2:42

Also see, Acts 6:4, which shows that it was "A praying church and a praying ministry!"[67] The whole church prayed and the leadership prayed "prayed continuously with steadfast determination".[68] If only churches would do that today, they could achieve anything, overcome any obstacle, and see countless souls saved, baptized, and filled with the Holy Spirit. But the wisdom and teaching of man has chosen a different route.

---

[65] Torrey, R.A. (2010-10-10). The Power of Prayer (Kindle Location 47-48). . Kindle Edition.

[66] Ibid. (pp. 58-59).
[67] Ibid. (pp. 77-78).
[68] Ibid. (p. 71).

Another Reason Churches and Christians Live Defeated and Struggling lives Today

"... [W]e do not live in a praying age. We live in an age of hustle and bustle, of man's efforts and man's determination, of man's confidence in himself and in his own power to achieve things, an age of human organization and human machinery, human push and human scheming, and human achievement, which in the things of God means no real achievement at all."[69]

Torrey wrote this over 100 years ago and it still applies today. The church has perfected itself to run smoothly and efficiently without the Holy Spirit's power. And when things don't go right, they come up with some new idea or twist or try to mimic successful churches that operate under the Holy Spirit's power. And some even do their best to mimic those who have no power but have ways of drawing large crowds. They simply shut out the Holy Spirit, dethrone Him, and mock Him by inserting His name here and there. If they really knew the Holy Spirit, they would tremble at the thought of grieving Him. But they don't know Him, nor do they know the Father or Jesus. They know of Them, but they truly don't know

[69] Ibid. (p. 88-91).

Them.

God Rewards Diligent and Persistent Seekers

"Prayer is the key that unlocks all the storehouses of God's infinite grace and power. All that God is, and all that God has, are at the disposal of prayer"[70]

> *"But without faith it is impossible to please him: for he that cometh to God must believe that he is, and that he is a rewarder of them that diligently seek him." Hebrews 11:6*

Torrey says that "the secret of Christians' Powerlessness" is based on the seven words found in James 4:2, *"Ye have not, because ye ask not."*[71] And he adds: the reasons Christians lack victory, make little progress in their life, win very few souls, or are unable to grow into the likeness of Christ is because of: "Neglect of prayer. You have not, because you ask not."[72]

He goes on to show that the same applies to ministers and churches in not seeing hardly any fruit, or are not seeing the progress and results in reaching the world and why they have so little victory over the world, the flesh and the devil.

---

[70] Ibid. (pp. 109-110).
[71] Ibid. (pp. 28-29).
[72] Ibid. (pp. 35-36)

Neglect of Holy Spirit led prayer and intercession leads to defeat and futility. How can such a church be triumphant, when it spends little or no time before the Lord? Without the Holy Spirit, there can be no Victory.

True Prayer Requires Sacrifice and Discipline

"Let the thought of this wondrous mystery of the nearness, the Indwelling, of the Holy God in you quiet your mind and heart into lowly fear and worship. Surrender the great enemy that opposes Him--the flesh, the self-life--day by day to Him to mortify and keep dead. Be content to aim at nothing less than being filled with the Spirit of the Man whose glory it is that He gave Himself to death to take away sin, with the whole being and doing under His control and inspiration. As your life in the Spirit becomes healthy and strong, as your spiritual constitution gets invigorated, your eye will see more clearly, your heart feel more keenly, what the sin around you is. Your thoughts and feelings will be those of the Holy Spirit breathing in you; your deep horror of sin, your deep faith in the redemption from it, your deep love to the souls who are in it, your willingness like your Lord to die if men can be freed from sin, will make you the fit instrument for the Spirit to convince the world of its sin."[73]

---

[73] Murray, Andrew (2010-06-01). The Spirit of Christ (Kindle Locations 1174-1181). . Kindle Edition

Many of us may have watched the Olympics and have heard the stories of how these athletes have spent hour upon hour every day practicing, giving up personal time and things they like, and how these days have turned into years, just so they could win a Gold Medal. In 1 Corinthians 9:24-27, Paul encourages us to run this race in order to obtain an "incorruptible crown." This race includes intercessory prayer and time with the Lord. Our strength to run this race comes from our surrendering to the will and leading of the Holy Spirit. How can we reflect Jesus or be like Him if we do not spend time alone with Him? How can we fulfill God's Will and His calling on our lives if we don't have fellowship with Him and know His voice? Many courses in world events have been changed by the Church's intercessory prayers. There is nothing more important in life and no greater priority than spending time in prayer with the Lord and interceding for others. We must ask the Holy Spirit to pray through us and to lead us into God's presence when we pray. It is upon His strength and not ours that we are able to "wait upon the Lord." Yes, we must make the choice to take time to pray. The Holy Spirit will help us quiet our heart and mind when we ask Him too. Surrender with your heart and not just your mind.

The Holy Spirit Will Give Us Compassion to Intercede for the Lost

In order to bring in the "sheaves" or to go out into the "highways and byways" and bring people into God's kingdom and house, it is important that we have a deep compassion for the Lost, the same as Jesus did. This compassion comes from our daily fellowship with the Lord and it grows as we surrender to the Holy Spirit in leading us to intercede for lost souls. When we are able to see the lost with compassion, as Jesus did, then our hearts will be burdened not only to pray for them, but also we will have a burden to witness to them. And our witness will be led by the Holy Spirit. He will give us the right words and scriptures at the right moment. These are also what I call "Divine Appointments."

We can only know God's voice and the Holy Spirit's leading from spending time alone with the Father and Son in our closet prayer time. It is in our closet prayer time that the Holy Spirit will teach us to pray fervently, to have faith in God, to seek Him diligently and will give us that assurance that God will reward us because we were diligent in seeking Him. The more we seek Him, the more we will know Him, the more we will love Him and the more we will want to spend time with Him. God's love and compassion will flow through us as never before.

If You Don't Spend Time with Jesus Now, Why Do You Want to Spend Eternity with Him later?

"And ye shall seek me, and find me, when ye shall search for me with all your heart." Jeremiah 29:13

"And thou shalt love the Lord thy God with all thy heart, and with all thy soul, and with all thy mind, and with all thy strength: this is the first commandment." Mark 12:30

"If ye love me, keep my commandments." John 14:15

"He that hath my commandments, and keepeth them, he it is that loveth me: and he that loveth me shall be loved of my Father, and I will love him, and will manifest myself to him." John 14:21

"If ye keep my commandments, ye shall abide in my love; even as I have kept my Father's commandments, and abide in his love." John 15:10

"Love not the world, neither the things that are in the world. If any man love the world, the love of the Father is not in him." 1 John 2:15

What will be the proof of our Love for the Lord when we stand before Him? Will He be a stranger to us or will He be a close friend, our Lord and our Master whom we love with every fiber of our being? Will He tell us just how much He loved the time we spent with Him in prayer? Or will He ask, "Why didn't you take time to get to know me?" Why do we Love Him?

Prayer should be a joy for us. In prayer, we are talking to the One Who Loves us beyond measure? Doesn't it make it easier for you to talk with someone who loves you and cares about you? In prayer, we can pour our heart out in confidence that He hears us and that He cares so very much about what is going on in our life and how we feel. By having the Holy Spirit praying through us, we can express ourselves to Him without fear of condemnation or retribution. He will make Himself known to us and we will feel His presence.

The world truly has nothing to offer us in life. This is not our home. In fact, the world for centuries has been dictating to the Church what acceptable Christianity is and there are those in the Church who have bowed and conformed to the world's form of Christianity. Jesus called the devil "the god of this world." He is the god of darkness and evil and those who don't belong to Jesus Christ are under his bondage. Yet, he is very good at getting Christians and Christian leaders to compromise or conform to the world's (his) idea of Christianity. Torrey says that he doesn't care if we pray, read the Bible or go to church, as long as we don't seek the Holy Ghost's power. As long as we don't spend time with Jesus and find other reasons to not to pray all that much or study God's

Word, then the devil has us just right where he wants us. There is no excuse for not spending time with Jesus.

Our closet prayer time is when we should fellowship with the Father and Son by the Holy Spirit. There is no such thing as "comfortable Christianity." Either we are on the battle field, with God's Armor, or we have succumbed to the devil's trickery that he will do us no harm. The devil doesn't want us to pray, nor does he want us to intercede for the lost or others. Is he winning that battle in your life?

CHAPTER 11: OUR NEED FOR THE HOLY SPIRIT

"And do not get drunk with wine, for that is debauchery; but ever be filled and stimulated with the [Holy] Spirit." Ephesians 5:18 (Amplified Bible)

The Holy Spirit Was Also Given Because of Our Weakness

Perhaps the main reason that there are so many doctrinal differences about the Holy Spirit is that many have forgotten why He was sent? As I said in the beginning of this study, that most Christian faiths believe that the Church began on the Day of Pentecost, when the Holy Spirit was outpoured upon those in the upper room. Beyond this belief there is a division among Christian faiths, which has brought about controversial, philosophical and theological debates about the Holy Spirit, His operation, the Gifts of the Spirit and so forth. Again, perhaps many have forgotten that the main reason He was sent was due to our human weakness and inability to fulfill our Lord's command to go out into the world and preach and teach the Gospel, as well as, to baptize, make disciples, heal the sick and so on? Even the disciples, who had been with Jesus and had gone at His command to preach the kingdom of God in surrounding villages, and to heal the sick and cast out demons, were told by our Lord that they needed to wait (in prayer) in Jerusalem until they were "endued" (which means "clothed") with power from on high[74] before they could obey His command to "Go." If those who walked with Jesus needed such power, then who are we to think otherwise? No one will ever be able to fulfill God's calling or command without the Holy Spirit. Yet, thousands go on trying every day.

Fruitful Branches

Andrew Murray in his book "The Vine" does a wonderful job detailing Jesus' parable and sermon on the Vine and Branches found in John 15. A branch cannot produce fruit on its own. It must be connected to the vine and the branch's life blood comes only from the vine. This life blood is the Holy Spirit. A branch cannot do anything on its own. It is totally dependent upon the vine. Still religion and vain religious philosophies teach that we can do things our own and that the more we try, the more God will honor us. I have got bad news for such thinkers and teachers: dead branches can never produce fruit, especially Spiritual fruit. Sure, a branch can be decorated and dressed up to look like a real branch, but

---

[74] Luke 24:29

it is still a dead branch. Why do so many ignore what Jesus said?

> *"Dwell in Me, and I will dwell in you. [Live in Me, and I will live in you.] Just as no branch can bear fruit of itself without abiding in (being vitally united to) the vine, neither can you bear fruit unless you abide in Me." John 15:4 (Amplified Bible).*

Can this promise and message be made any clearer? Without being attached to Jesus and without the Holy Spirit flowing into us, not only will we never produce the fruit that God desires, but we will remain dead branches, useless to God and to the world around us. I didn't say this, Jesus said it.

The Gift of the Holy Spirit

> *"I indeed baptize you with water unto repentance. but he that cometh after me is mightier than I, whose shoes I am not worthy to bear: he shall baptize you with the Holy Ghost, and with fire:" Matthew 3:11*

> *"For John truly baptized with water; but ye shall be baptized with the Holy Ghost not many days hence". Acts 1:5*

As already mentioned in this book, the gift of the Holy Spirit and the baptism with the Holy Spirit are the same thing. Torrey makes a lengthy case in his book that "the baptism with the Holy Spirit is an operation of the Holy Spirit distinct from and additional to His regenerating work."[75]   He adds, "the baptism with the Holy Spirit is the birthright of every believer."[76] When one is baptized with the Holy Spirit, there is a Spiritual transformation that takes place and the one baptized receives a great boldness and desire to share Jesus. This has been proven over the centuries through the lives of Wesley, Finney, Moody, Brainerd, Murray, Torrey, T.L. Osborn and countless thousands upon thousands. Everyone one of these men who were baptized with the Holy Spirit was used mightily by God. These men's writings are still read by thousands today. The Holy Spirit's anointing lives on in their writings.

John Wesley Countered Unbelief Against the Holy Spirit

I didn't know how John Wesley felt about the Holy Spirit and the Gifts of the Spirit, until I read an article recently, entitled, "John Wesley and the Gifts of the Holy Spirit."[77] The author. Robert Tuttle,   tells how John Wesley

---

[75] Torrey, R. A. (Reuben Archer) (2011-03-24). The Person and Work of The Holy Spirit (pp. 100-101). . Kindle Edition.

[76] Ibid. (Kindle Locations p. 102).

believed in the gifts of the Holy Spirit and why they were withdrawn from the Early Church.

"I was fully convinced of what I had long suspected, 1. That the Montanists, in the second and third centuries, were real, scriptural Christians; and, 2. that the grand reason why the miraculous gifts were so soon withdrawn, was not only that faith and holiness were well nigh lost; but that dry, formal, orthodox men began even then to ridicule whatever gifts they had not themselves, and to decry them all as either madness or imposture."

Wesley also wrote that the reason the Gifts of the Spirit had ceased under Constantine was due to the fact "there was no more occasion for them,' because all the world was become Christians." And he also said, "This was the real cause why the extraordinary gifts of the Holy Ghost were no longer to be found in the Christian Church; because the Christians were turned Heathens again, and had only a dead form left." Tuttle goes on to argue, "...the fact remains that Wesley believed that the gifts of the Holy Spirit were not only important but also were active during the 18th century Evangelical Revival." Are these not also some of the same reasons used today to deny the Gift of the Holy Spirit and the Gifts of the Spirit? Without the Holy Spirit, a church is dead.

---

[77] http://www.ucmpage.org/articles/rtuttle1.html

Not everyone is Baptized with the Holy Spirit in the Same Way

"If ye then, being evil, know how to give good gifts unto your children: how much more shall your heavenly Father give the Holy Spirit to them that ask him?" Luke 11:3

The book of Acts shows various ways people were baptized with the Holy Spirit. Besides the laying on of hands or the preaching of the Gospel, Jesus said that the Holy Spirit would be given unto everyone who asks the Father to baptize them with the Holy Spirit. Here Jesus is speaking about the "gift of the Holy Spirit" that was to come after His ascension into heaven. Asking and believing go hand in hand. Taking God at His Word in faith produces results. Those who ask will receive. Torrey says that after we ask, then we are to believe we have received it and move forward. The evidence that we have received it may come in a short period of time or at a later time. We are simply to believe that we have received what Jesus promised.

I heard, Jack Hayford, President of the Foursquare International Church, tell how it took him five years to receive the baptism. He struggled with receiving it. Others have had this same struggle.

Torrey says that unbelief, as well as sin not repented of will keep us from being baptized. If we hold grudges, unforgiveness, have any form of pride or are living sinful lives, then the Holy Spirit will not fill unclean vessels. This explains to me, why some who sought the baptism didn't receive it. The Holy Spirit is Holy. He will fill surrendered lives. Again, all we need to do is ask God to Baptize us with the Holy Spirit. Jesus promised that He would.

I have been in both Pentecostal and non-Pentecostal churches. I understand their doctrinal differences on the Holy Spirit. The non-Pentecostals don't want to be like the Pentecostals because of the way they openly worship or speak-in-tongues and the way they strongly emphasize the Holy Spirit and His Gifts. On the other hand, the Pentecostals, for the most part, look down upon those who don't worship the way they do, or speak-in-tongues, or manifest the Holy Spirit's Gifts. This shouldn't be in either case.

Those who are "filled" with the Spirit don't go around doing crazy things. It is true the Corinthian church got carried away at one time, but Paul set them straight. Yet, the non-Pentecostals, for the most part, want to label all Pentecostals as being like the Corinthian church. They're not. What being filled with the Holy Spirit means is to be filled with the fullness of God. Why would we not want that as Christians? We can' just have God, or just have Jesus, and or just have the Holy

Spirit. God, Jesus and the Holy Spirit are inseparable.[78] Where One is, the other two are also present.

Being baptized with the Holy Spirit (i.e. receiving the Gift of the Holy Spirit) is simply part of the salvation process, just as much as is being baptized with water.[79] Read Acts and the writings of Paul, Peter and John; they all agree on the importance of being filled with the Holy Spirit.[80] Being filled with the Spirit is not something anyone should be afraid of; instead those who desire to draw closer to the Lord will find it a necessity and a wonderful experience. The Holy Spirit does not cause us to boast, act proud or to look down upon others. Instead the Holy Spirit is gentle, kind, patient and leads us into a wonderful and beautiful relationship with the Father and Son. He is our Guide, our Comforter and our Teacher.[81] We need Him every moment of our life. Without the Holy Spirit we cannot truly live a Christian life or be pleasing unto the Lord. Simply ask Jesus to fill you with the Holy Spirit. He has promised to do it.[82]

---

[78] Saint Ambrose Books on the Holy Spirit.
[79] Acts 2:38
[80] Mark 1:8; Acts 1:5; and Acts 2:38
[81] John 14:26
[82] Luke 11:13

The Difference between the Gifts of the Spirit and Human Talents

"⁴ Now there are diversities of gifts, but the same Spirit.

⁵ And there are differences of administrations, but the same Lord.

⁶ And there are diversities of operations, but it is the same God which worketh all in all.

⁷ But the manifestation of the Spirit is given to every man to profit withal.

⁸ For to one is given by the Spirit the word of wisdom; to another the word of knowledge by the same Spirit;

⁹ To another faith by the same Spirit; to another the gifts of healing by the same Spirit;

¹⁰ To another the working of miracles; to another prophecy; to another discerning of spirits; to another divers kinds of tongues; to another the interpretation of tongues:

¹¹ But all these worketh that one and the selfsame

*Spirit, dividing to every man severally as he will." 1
Corinthians 12*

There are only 9 gifts of the Holy Spirit: Word of wisdom; word of knowledge; faith; gifts of healing(s); working of miracles; prophecy; discerning(s) of spirits; various types of tongues; and interpretation of tongues. Every other talented gift that we may have is not a gift of the Holy Spirit. Like I said earlier, He doesn't do our bidding. The gifts are not for our personal use and benefit. They are given and to be used for "edifying of the Church." 1 Corinthians 14:12.

Besides the gifts being manifested inside the Church, outside of the Church the working of miracles, (signs and wonders) and the gifts of healings and the discerning of spirits often accompany anointed ministers and ministries when Jesus Christ and the Gospel is being preached to the unsaved and heathen. The majority of churches that Paul founded were with the manifestation and demonstration of the power of the Holy Spirit took place. (The Galatian church was founded in such manner.) Where there is a praying church and where the Holy Spirit has control, then the gifts of the Spirit will be evident. Those who are given gifts should be humbled by the fact that the Holy Spirit chose to give them such gifts or manifest Himself through them. The gifts are given because of our inabilities to fulfill God's Plan for the Church.

The Misuse of the Gifts

It is a sad thing to see people become prideful and possessive of the gifts of the Spirit. Where there is pride there is no love. Spiritual pride leads to deception and all kind of errors. The Holy Spirit does not manifest Himself in those with spiritual pride or who are possessive with the gift they were first given. There are those who beg and plead as well as demand that the Holy Spirit perform signs and wonders in their midst. He doesn't answer such self-seeking prayer. Whatever is manifested definitely is not the Holy Spirit. The Holy Spirit never does anything against scripture. If people are led to do things or say things that are contrary to scripture, it is not the Holy Spirit leading them.

Those who confuse talents and abilities with spiritual gifts simply don't know the Holy Spirit. We can't discern our gifts by a checklist. The word manifestation means that the Holy Spirit chooses when, where and how He will manifest Himself. The gifts of the spirit are not there for our everyday use. Yes, He does give specific gifts to those who are in the ministry. Yet they are given because of our weakness and inability to fulfill God's call on our life.

There are No Inferior Gifts of the Spirit

"Every good gift and every perfect gift is from above, and cometh down from the Father of lights, with whom is no variableness, neither shadow of turning."

James 1:17

"⁷ But the manifestation of the Spirit is given to every man to profit withal." 1 Corinthians 12

Some erringly believe that in 1 Corinthians 14, Paul is speaking against the use of tongues and therefore they conclude that it is an inferior and not needed gift. The Holy Spirit doesn't give inferior gifts or lessor gifts. Praying in the Spirit in tongues is the Holy Spirit praying through us and for us to God. As a result our inner man is built up. Paul clearly boasted that he spoke in tongues than most of them in the Corinthian church and wish that they all did the same. If tongues were inferior or a lessor gift, then why would Paul go on speaking in tongues? What some get confused at here is that Paul is simply saying that, when we are gathered together that prophesying in their own language is better for the edifying of the church; however, the exception is that when the Holy Spirit speaks through someone in tongues and via the Holy Spirit one interprets the message in tongues, then the church also is edified. Further, if tongues were inferior, Paul would not have said, "Forbid not the speaking in tongues." Yet, so many churches disobey this command.

CHAPTER 12: BE HOLY

"According as he hath chosen us in him before the foundation of the world, that we should be holy and without blame before him in love:" Ephesians 1:4

Holiness Only Comes From God

Holiness is not an attribute that we can obtain on our own. Wherever God is present so is His Holiness. Jesus came to make us Holy so that a Holy God could dwell in us via His Holy Spirit. When we are converted we become new creatures [a new creation] in Christ.[83] Our bodies become a Holy Temple for the Holiness, power and fullness of God to dwell in. When we sin, especially with our bodies, we sin not only against God, but we grieve the Holy Spirit Who dwells within in us and we defile our body that has been made a Holy Temple.[84] We usually don't think about this defilement when we sin, but once we realize that we have defiled ourselves, we should immediately confess our sin, repent of it and ask God to forgive us. Our sin prohibits God and all His fullness from operating in our lives. Many forget that God is a Jealous God,

---

[83] 2 Corinthians 5:17
[84] 1 Corinthians 6:19

and He wants all of us unto Himself.[85] He loves us beyond measure and His jealousy is justified.

Faithful

When we choose to live life our way and not seek to follow God's Way, we become like an unfaithful spouse. While society may wink at unfaithfulness, God does not. Holiness has no part in sin or darkness. A True loving spouse has the right to become jealous if anyone or anything diverts the true love and devotion between his or her spouse. And like a True loving spouse, God is more than willing to forgive and restore that loving relationship. He desires to be intimate with us and to have us be Holy as He is Holy.[86] Jesus paid the price through cruel crucifixion on the cross and by the shedding of His precious and Holy Blood, so that we could have a Holy and Eternal relationship with Him and the Father. We were redeemed by the Blood of the Lamb,[87] a costly price, and therefore Our Father should be jealous when our attention is turned away from Him. The Church is the Bride of Christ and God desires that His Son only have the most Holy and Glorious Bride. Therefore, God's jealousy is a righteous and Holy jealousy.

Be Holy

Again God's requirement for us to be Holy is not obtained by our own actions or deeds. We are Holy when God

---

[85] Exodus 34:14
[86] John 14:23
[87] Galatians 3:13; 1 Peter 1:18; and Revelation 5:9

dwells fully in us by His Holy Spirit. Our failings and weaknesses don't prevent us from being Holy as long as we continually confess and repent of them. Holiness is not something we should look for in ourselves, only others will see it. We should never be satisfied with the thought that we have obtained perfect Holiness; instead we should continually humble ourselves before the Lord and admit that only He is Holy.[88] It is only by and through the Holy Spirit that we can be Holy. A Holy people make up a Holy Church and that is what the Lord Jesus is coming back for. Do people around us see and sense God's Holiness in us?

---

[88] Matthew 18:14; James 4:10; and 1 Peter 5:6

CHAPTER 13: LET JESUS CHRIST LIVE THROUGH YOU

"But be ye doers of the word, and not hearers only, deceiving your own selves." James 1:22

Good Works

Good Works should be an automatic result of our relationship and walk with the Lord. *"Faith without works is dead"*,[89] James clearly writes in this second chapter. There are people who do nice and charitable things for others because it is in their nature to do so. However, Godly Good Works go beyond our nature, they are actions that are inspired by God's love and the Holy Spirit within us. Some believe that by doing good works on their own will help them win God's love, grace or favor. Nothing could be further from the truth. Others do good works in order to get recognition and praise from men. This is vanity and God does not bless it. When we have a true relationship with the Jesus and the Father, then we will also have a love and compassion for others. We will freely give

---

[89] James 2

because we have freely received from God His Love and Mercy and Grace. This also applies to the Church.

Good and Faithful Servants

Jesus in Matthew 25 gives a parable about the talents given to His servants and how He expects them to go out and multiply those talents. Those who obey He calls them; "good and faithful servants" and they inherit eternal life. And we know about the one servant who hid his talent and how the Lord rebuked Him and cast him out into "outer darkness." In reality, this parable should be a rude awakening for all of us who follow Christ. Our salvation is not something we are to keep to ourselves. The Church should not isolate itself from the world, as some have done, and seek God's blessings and goodness only for themselves. Our Lord is not coming back for such a church. We are to be living witnesses to those around us; not in word only, but in word and deed. Our actions should demonstrate what we believe and in Whom we believe. As a result, our words and actions will prove that Jesus Christ lives in us and will cause others to want to know Him too. This is how our talents are to be multiplied. This is God's Divine Plan for His Church.

Blessed of My Father

"34 Then shall the King say unto them on his right hand, Come, ye blessed of my Father, inherit the

kingdom prepared for you from the foundation of the world:

35 For I was an hungered, and ye gave me meat: I was thirsty, and ye gave me drink: I was a stranger, and ye took me in:

36 Naked, and ye clothed me: I was sick, and ye visited me: I was in prison, and ye came unto me.

37 Then shall the righteous answer him, saying, Lord, when saw we thee an hungred, and fed thee? or thirsty, and gave thee drink?

38 When saw we thee a stranger, and took thee in? or naked, and clothed thee?

39 Or when saw we thee sick, or in prison, and came unto thee?

40 And the King shall answer and say unto them, Verily I say unto you, Inasmuch as ye have done it unto one of the least of these my brethren, ye have done it unto me." Matthew 25

To all the Christians and churches that are fulfilling God's vision of Matthew 25:35 & 36, praise God. To the rest I must ask, "Why not?" True some are physically unable to do these things, yet nearly all of us are at least able to donate and financially support those in who do in some way or form. More than that, we all can and should intercede and prayerfully support all that do. Yet, there is more to this.

The Holy Spirit's or Self-Motivation?

Charities that do these things are much needed. Yet, just how many are doing these things because they have God's love in their hearts? Are there Christians and churches doing all or some of these things because it is the right thing to do, or are they doing it because the Holy Spirit has led them to do these things? Is there a difference? Yes there is. It is either being done by self-motivation or by the Holy Spirit's leading. Self-motivation leads to boasting and the seeking of man's praise. The Holy Spirit's leading seeks no rewards or recognition but gladly gives all unto the Lord. Eternal rewards await those who are doing these things by the Holy Spirit's leading. Isn't that what we are to look forward to receiving?

Don't Forget the Gospel Message

History has shown that many who have done such good works under the Holy Spirit's leading start off with preaching the Gospel while doing these good works. But somewhere down the road the good works became the priority and the Gospel Message became less important or was simply diminished to a "God Bless You" as the charity supplied the needs. A good of example of that is the Church in China.

When the missionaries went in they preached the gospel and built churches. Then they built hospitals and schools. After a while, the Gospel was less preached and the main focus became taking care of the poor, sick and needy. The Chinese people no longer heard the Gospel message. In the 1930's and 1940's, it didn't take long for the Communist party to recruit members. They broadcast their teachings on radio and in person, while the church stood by and kept on doing what it had been doing. By the end of the 1940's missionaries were forced out of China.

What good is it to feed and clothe people, visit the sick, visit those in prison and take in strangers and so forth and never tell them about Jesus and the Good News? Are we simply required to do these things and hope that somewhere down the line that they will find God? Does anyone know whether or not that person or persons that they are helping will live beyond today? Are we ashamed of our Lord Jesus Christ, Who freely gave His life for us? Will we silently allow people to continue their path to eternal death and be satisfied with the thought that we met some physical or emotional need? How can we stand before the Lord and expect to be called "ye blessed of My Father" when we never mentioned Jesus and the Good News to those we have helped? Salvation does not come by osmosis or wishful thinking.

People are dying each day who don't know Jesus by the tens of thousands. Are we as a Church going to continue to let them die by choosing to remain silent or by only being concerned about their physical needs? Why are we Christians? Why do we serve the Lord? Why do we go to Church? Are we and our church fulfilling God's call, His commands and vision for His Church? If not, then is it not time that we become obedient to God's vision? Is it not also about time that we seek to be His Glorious Church that we may live out our lives the way the Father meant for us to live? We are the Church! Let us pray and desire that we become the Church Triumphant! Let us also pray, "Lord, here am I. Fill me with your Holy Spirit and lead me, so that I may be obedient to Your Will. Amen."

CHAPTER 14: GOD'S DIVINE PLAN FOR HIS GLORIOUS CHURCH

God's Divine Plan for His Glorious Church, is that His Church be built upon Jesus Christ as the Corner Stone, with the Prophets and Apostles as the foundation. The Church didn't officially come into existence until the day of Pentecost, when the Holy Spirit was outpoured in power. The Church began Pentecostal and God's Divine Plan is for the Church to remain Pentecostal. As we know, men with hardened hearts and self-seeking desires crept in bringing with them all kinds of heresies and bondages, aiding the work of Satan to destroy the Church. Yet, the Church cannot be destroyed.

God's Divine Plan for you and me is that Jesus Christ and the Fullness of the Godhead dwell in and live in us by the power of the Holy Spirit. His plan includes our total dependence upon Him via the Holy Spirit and that we not only walk in the Spirit but every minute of our life we are to be led by the Spirit. God not only wants to reveal Himself to us, but He desires to communicate and fellowship with us as His Children. He not only wants us to know His love, but also for us to have His Love shed abroad in our hearts by the Holy Spirit, so that the world around us will know His love as well.

Through Jesus Christ and His shed blood, God made a way for us to spend eternity with Them. We were created in His image, and through Jesus Christ we can be made into His likeness.

God's Divine Plan is that the Church be a Church of prayer, a Church filled with power, love, good works, a Church that is Holy and Glorious; a Church that is Triumphant. Jesus is coming back for His spotless (free from sin and the world's corruption) Bride. That is why Jesus, Paul, the Saints and countless others beg us to put off our former desires and way of living, so that we may inherit Eternal Life. Without Jesus life is simply not worth living.

Jesus has kept His promise not to forsake us or leave us. The Father sent the Holy Spirit so that Jesus could live in us and through us. God sent the Holy Spirit as Our Comforter, our guide, the One who stays by our side, the one who teaches us all things, who brings things to our remembrance, the one who tells of things to come, the one who empowers us, and the one who intercedes for us with groanings and utterances and much, much more. How can we ignore Him or grieve Him?

Oh, I could write so much more. In the future, with the Holy Spirit's guidance, I may write more and explain more. However, let me encourage you to begin reading books by Andrew Murray and R.A. Torrey and others listed at the end of this book. I have studied some of these books and re-read them over and over again along with the Word of God for nearly the past 20 years. And yet, I have not learned all there is to know.

If you seek God, you will find Him and He will reveal Himself to you. If you ask Him to teach you, He will by His Holy Spirit. If you ask Jesus to teach you how to pray, He will via the Holy Spirit. Learn to ask the Holy Spirit to pray through you each time you pray. Learn to ask the Holy Spirit to speak to you as you read the Word and anointed books.

God's Divine Plan for His Glorious Church includes you! If you are not yet part of His Church, you can be today. Ask God to forgive you in Jesus name. Ask Him to make Himself real to you. He will. Find a Bible Believing, Holy Spirit filled Church. It is never too late to turn to God.

Humbly In Christ Jesus,

Lonnie Brown

ABOUT THE AUTHOR

At age 15, Lonnie Brown felt the call of God on his life to go into the ministry. He never told anyone; however, Evangelist Dick Mills publically confirmed the calling. Mr. Brown wasn't sure what the calling meant. He did end up pastoring a few small churches and youth pastored another. Yet, somehow this wasn't his calling.

After going through many years of personal struggle, heartaches and defeat, the Holy Spirit revealed to him that his calling was to write, teach and do one-on-one ministering.

For nearly 20 years Lonnie read and re-read Andrew Murray's books. It wasn't until the last 5 years before writing this book, that these books, along with scripture and other writings mentioned in here became real to him. Lonnie found that the answers to many of his personal struggles lay in allowing the Holy Spirit to regenerate and transform his life. When this regeneration and transformation took place, everything else in Lonnie's life began to change and doors opened up for him to write, teach and do one-on-one ministry. This is still ongoing in his life.

He does not seek to become famous or wealthy via his writings. It took him nearly a lifetime of searching to come to the Spiritual knowledge and understandings that are briefly written in this book. Under the Holy Spirit's inspiration and guidance, he has chosen to share some of what he has learned, so that those also seeking may come to the knowledge of the truth, especially about God's Divine Plan for His Church and His Children. He takes no credit for anything written herein.

BIBLIOGRAPHY

And Sources Relied Upon and Recommended Readings:

Scripture Verses taken from www.BibleGateway.com

William Law
A Serious Call to a Devout and Holy Life
_____
Books by Andrew Murray:
Also available in Kindle e-books:

The Master's Indwelling
The Ministry of Intercession A Plea for More Prayer
Divine Healing
Lord Teach Us To Pray
Jesus Himself
Holy In Christ Thoughts on the Calling of God's Children to be Holy
The Spirit of Christ
The Vine

_____
Books by R.A. Torrey: Also available in Kindle e-books
The Person and Work of the Holy Spirit
The Power of Prayer
_____

Dick Mills: *The 4 Loves*
_____

T.L. Osborn, *The Message That Works*
You may read more writings by Lonnie at

http://wwwAboveAllPower.com

www.ingramcontent.com/pod-product-compliance
Lightning Source LLC
Chambersburg PA
CBHW060510030426
42337CB00015B/1831